gifts *in* jars

80 QUICK & EASY HANDMADE FOOD PRESENTS **FOR ANY BUDGET**

CASSIE JOHNSTON

Gifts in Jars: 80 Quick & Easy Handmade Food Presents for Any Budget
Copyright © 2024 Cassie Johnston. All rights reserved.
Published by Cassie Johnston / Back to Her Roots, LLC
ISBN 979-8-9916691-0-8

Cover Design: Cassie Johnston
Photographers: Cassie Johnston, Steve Cukrov, Brent Hofacker, Becky Winkler
Editor: Julie Grice

table of contents

introduction **4**
about the jars **6**
packaging for gifting **11**

BAKING MIXES 16

- Brownie Mix **18**
- Cranberry Orange Muffin Mix **20**
- Double Chocolate Muffin Mix **22**
- Confetti Cake Mix **24**
- Gingerbread Cookie Mix **26**
- M&M Cookie Mix **28**
- Snickerdoodle Cookie Mix **30**
- Gluten-Free Chocolate Chip Cookie Mix **32**
- Whole Grain Pancake Mix **34**
- Gluten-Free Pancake Mix **36**

SALTY SNACKS 38

- Popcorn Seasonings **40**
- Rosemary Party Nuts **42**
- Sweet and Spicy Mixed Nuts **44**
- Trail Mixes **46**
- Cheese Straws **48**
- Roasted Chickpeas **50**
- Nuts 'n' Bolts **52**

SWEET SNACKS 54

- Sea Salt Honey Caramels **56**
- Peppermint Bark **58**
- Edible Cookie Dough **60**
- Cranberry Pistachio Bark **62**
- Peanut Butter Chocolate Chip Granola **64**
- Buckeyes **66**
- Turtles **68**
- Puppy Chow **70**

DRINKS 72

- Cappuccino Mix **74**
- Golden Milk Mix **76**
- Loose Leaf Chai **78**
- Hot Cocoa Mix **80**
- Coffee Liqueur **82**
- Cranberry Liqueur **84**
- Limoncello **86**
- Cocktail Kits **88**
- Irish Cream **90**

FOR THE COOK 92

- Grill Seasonings **94**
- Everything Bagel Seasoning **96**
- Ranch Seasoning & Dressing Mix **98**
- Infused Finishing Salts **100**
- Vanilla Extract **102**
- Sun-Dried Tomatoes **104**
- Infused Olive Oil **106**
- Flavored Sugars **108**
- Quick Hot Sauce **110**
- Peeled Garlic **112**

DINNERS 114

- Coconut Curry Soup Mix **116**
- Black Bean Soup Mix **118**
- Split Pea Soup Mix **120**
- Chicken Noodle Soup Mix **122**
- Three-Bean Chili Mix **124**
- Five-Bean Soup Mix **126**
- Italian Barley Soup Mix **128**
- Garlic & Herb Pizza Crust Mix **130**
- Gluten-Free Pizza Crust Mix **132**

CANNED GOODS 134

- Canning Basics **136**
- Berry Syrups **140**
- Bourbon Peach Jam **142**
- Pomegranate Jelly **144**
- Spiced Apple Butter **146**
- Red Onion Jam **148**
- Mustard Flight **150**
- Pickled Beets **154**

acknowledgements **157**
about the author **159**
index **160**

RECIPE LEGEND

introduction

In a world that can feel fast-paced and impersonal at times, there's something incredibly heartfelt about giving—and receiving—a handmade gift.

But I know what you're probably thinking: who has the time or the money to make handmade gifts? Well, I've got some good news. Here in *Gifts in Jars*, I'm sharing with you over 80 edible treasures that are not only thoughtful but also easy to make and affordable for any budget. In fact, the vast majority of the gifts in these pages can be made in under five minutes for under five dollars each.

From savory snacks to sweet spreads, each recipe is designed to be beautifully packaged in affordable and easy-to-source canning jars. Because the jars are reusable, the contents are consumable, and the wrapping is low waste, this method of gift-giving can be a wonderful contrast to the overabundance that sometimes feels like it overpowers the spirit of gift-giving.

So whether you're looking to give a thoughtful holiday gift, thank a special teacher, or congratulate someone on their new home, these jarred goodies are the perfect solution to all your gift-giving needs. With each jar you create, you're not just making food—you're sharing a piece of your heart.

3-Bean Chili Mix

Slow Cooker Directions: Brown 1 pound of ground beef, drain fat, and then combine the beef with the chili mix, 12 cups of water, 1 can of diced tomatoes, and 1 can of tomato paste in a slow cooker and cook on high for 8 hours until beans are tender.

Instant Pot Directions: Brown 1 pound of ground beef, drain fat, and then combine the beef with the chili mix, 12 cups of water, 1 can diced tomatoes, and 1 can tomato paste in the Instant Pot. Seal and cool on Manual/High for 30 minutes with a natural press release.

about the jars

Wide-mouth, regular-mouth, pint, quart—if you're new to the world of canning jars, it can feel like you have to learn a whole new language! Don't worry, let me be your translator.

JAR SIZES

Every gift in this book is packaged in standard-size mason canning jars. I offer suggestions for which jars I like to use for each recipe, but you are welcome to experiment with what size jars work best for you. The only section of the book where you can't change jar sizes is the Canned Goods section (page 134)—that's because using the right jar size is important for safety of the final product when water bath canning. Otherwise, let your creativity shine!

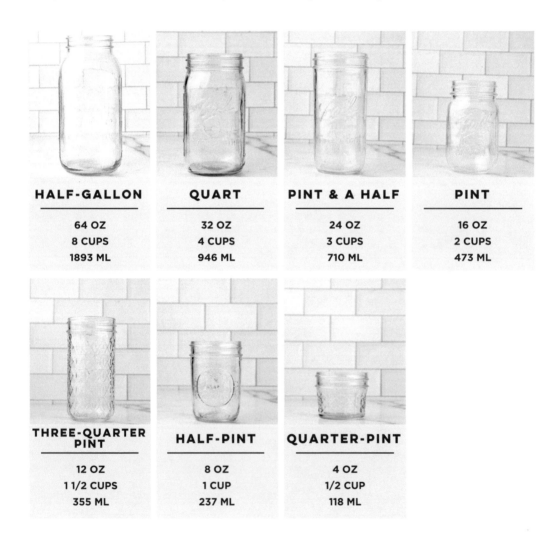

HALF-GALLON	QUART	PINT & A HALF	PINT
64 OZ	32 OZ	24 OZ	16 OZ
8 CUPS	4 CUPS	3 CUPS	2 CUPS
1893 ML	946 ML	710 ML	473 ML

THREE-QUARTER PINT	HALF-PINT	QUARTER-PINT
12 OZ	8 OZ	4 OZ
1 1/2 CUPS	1 CUP	1/2 CUP
355 ML	237 ML	118 ML

REGULAR MOUTH (ACTUAL SIZE)

⟵ ⟶

2 3/8" INNER DIAMETER

REGULAR MOUTH VS. WIDE MOUTH

Most canning jars come in one of two different opening widths—regular mouth or wide mouth. In general, you can choose whichever you have on hand or is easiest for you to source. If I have to choose between the two, I recommend wide mouth for the majority of the projects in this book simply because the wider opening makes the jars easier to fill.

WIDE MOUTH (ACTUAL SIZE)

⟵ ⟶

3" INNER DIAMETER

protip

Make sure to grab the right size lid when purchasing new lids for your jars! Regular mouth lids will not fit on wide mouth jars, and vice versa.

Gluten Free
Pizza Crust

Mixed Nuts

Cappuccino
Mix

HANDMADE WITH

3-Bean
Chili Mix

Slow Cooker Directions: Brown 1 pound of
ground beef, drain fat, and then combine the
beef with the chili mix, 12 cups of water, 1 can
of diced tomatoes, and 1 can of tomato paste
in a slow cooker and cook on high for 8 hours
until beans are tender.

Instant Pot Directions: Brown 1 pound of
ground beef, drain fat, and then combine the
beef with the chili mix, 12 cups of water, 1 can
diced tomatoes, and 1 can tomato paste in the
Instant Pot. Seal and cool on Manual/High for
30 minutes with a natural press release.

Double
Chocolate
MUFFIN M

Cranberry
Liqueur

MADE WITH VODKA

SOURCING NEW CANNING JARS

If you've never purchased canning jars before, you might be surprised how easy it is to find them! While you can purchase them online, shipping usually is quite expensive due to the weight and shipping cost (or the seller will markup the sale price to account for it). My preferred place to buy new canning jars is my local hardware store. Most keep a small section of canning supplies all year, with the section growing much larger in the summer months. You can also purchase canning jars are most major big box stores (like Target and Walmart) and many supermarkets.

SOURCING USED CANNING JARS

The great thing about canning jars is that if you take good care of them, they will last generations. I have hundreds of jars that were passed down to me from my parents, who got them from my grandparents! If you don't have a family hookup like I do, canning jars are often found on tables at flea markets, yard sales, and auctions for pennies on the dollar. A good washing and they look as good as new!

protip

There is a robust community of mason jar collectors, so if you are at a flea market and see a jar with a hefty price tag on it, it's probably because it's a rare or antique jar. Those jars are beautiful to admire, but not the right fit for our affordable gift-making purposes.

UPCYCLING JARS

Do you have to use standard canning jars for gift-giving? Absolutely not! I love a good upcycle moment, and many of these gifts look just as beautiful in an upcycled spaghetti sauce jar as they do in a new canning jar. Not only are you saving money, but you're also giving new life to something that was destined for the recycling bin.

If you do want to upcycle jars for your gift-giving, here are a few tips:

- Choose a jar with a tight-fitting lid—especially if working with liquids. Spaghetti sauce jars are some of my favorites.
- A hairdryer and rubbing alcohol is my favorite way to remove sticky labels from upcycled jars! I warm the label with my hair dryer until it peels off, then clean up any sticky residue with a cotton ball soaked in rubbing alcohol.
- Know that upcycled jars don't have standard sizes, so you might have to do some trial and error to see which recipe fits in which jar.
- Do NOT use upcycled jars for any of the items in the Canned Goods section (page 134). It's important to use jars and lids made specifically for canning for safety reasons.

JAR ETIQUETTE

Don't be surprised if the jar you gift ends up back in your hands! Especially in rural communities, it's considered good etiquette to return the empty (and clean) jar to the gift-giver once you've enjoyed the contents. Personally, I never expect the jar back—if my giftee finds a use for the jar, that's wonderful!—but I am appreciative when I do get it back.

CANNING JAR LIDS

When you purchase a new canning jar, it will come with a two-piece canning lid—a flat lid and a ring that attaches the lid to the jar. These lids are watertight, safe for canning, and easy to use. The majority of the jars in this book are closed using these lids, and you don't need to stray beyond those lids if you don't want to. But, like most things in life, there are options! Some of these lids will be available at your local store where you source canning jars (see page 9), but many are also available at online retailers.

Two-Piece Canning Lid

The standard lid that comes with all jars. These are the only lids safe for water bath canning (see the Canned Goods section on page 134 for more information). They are watertight.

Wooden Storage Lids

These beautiful lids are best for dry goods, as they have a tendency to pop off somewhat easily.

Plastic Storage Lids

These are the best lids I've found for items that are liquid or otherwise might corrode a metal lid over time (like the Peeled Garlic gift on page 112). I've seen them mostly in white, gray, and black.

Metal Storage Lids

These look a lot like the two-piece canning lids but are all contained in one piece and are not safe for water bath canning. They come in a wide variety of colors.

packaging for gifting

The beauty of gifts in jars, in large part, lies in their simplicity. You don't need to make your jars particularly fancy or complicated—unless that brings you joy—but a few small steps can make a simple jar feel incredibly special.

JAR WRAPPING IDEAS

I'm going to be honest, my favorite way to wrap a jar for gift-giving is to tie a simple ribbon around it with a pretty tag and call it a day! But that's just one of many options for how to fancy up your jar for gifting.

Ribbon or Twine

It takes less than 30 seconds, but tying on a brightly colored strip of ribbon, twine, or even leather strap can help your gift jars feel even more special. I recommend sticking with ribbon that is less than an inch in width—it's easier to work with around the neck of the jar. Both small bows and simple double knots look great on jars. I tend to rely on double knots a lot because bows can be tricky to get to cooperate sometimes!

COTTON RIBBON (7/8")

WAXED JEWELRY CORD

SUEDE STRAPPING

BAKER'S TWINE

JUTE TWINE

SATIN RIBBON (1/2")

Fabric Circles

Topping gift jars with scrap fabric makes a jar feel thoughtful and special. You can use scrap fabric from anyhwere—old pillowcases, t-shirts, or flannels. Or if you are looking for modern patterns, purchase fat quarters (pre-cut pieces of 18″ x 22″ fabric available at fabric and craft stores).

STEP 1

Using a salad bowl or saucer, trace a circle on the wrong side of the fabric. I've found a 6″ to 7″ bowl works perfectly for both wide-mouth and regular-mouth jars.

STEP 2

Cut out the circle using pinking shears or scallop shears. You can use regular scissors, but the pinking or scallop sheers help to prevent the fabric from fraying.

STEP 3

Place the fabric circle over top of the jar, and use a small, color-coordinated rubber band to attach it. You can also skip the rubber band and just use the ring of the canning lid to secure the fabric to the jar.

STEP 4

Tie a piece of ribbon, twine, or leather strap over top of the rubber band.

Tea Towel Wrapping

Furoshiki is the traditional Japanese art of wrapping gifts in cloth, and while wrapping a jar in a tea towel isn't spot-on to tradition, the method I show here is very much inspired by the practice. I love this method of jar wrapping because it's beautiful, zero-waste, and thoughtful. I like to collect tea towels throughout the year that remind me of my friends and family—that way I have a constant supply of fun and varying "wrapping papers" to use.

STEP 1

Place a large tea towel on a flat surface wrong-side up. Square-ish towels are easier to work with than rectangular towels. Place your closed jar in the middle of the towel.

STEP 2

Pull up opposing corners of the towel and tie into a knot on top of the jar.

STEP 3

Pull up the other set of opposing corners, and gather any edges of the towel that remain.

STEP 4

Using a rubber band, secure the bundle at the top of the jar like you're securing a ponytail.

STEP 5

Tie a piece of ribbon, twine, or leather strap over top of the rubber band.

TAGS

The final step to preparing your jars for gifting is to label them. I highly recommend labeling them so not only do you know what's in them, but your giftee does too! I know it's easy to think you'll remember, but all it takes is one mix-up of Hot Sauce (page 110) and Strawberry Syrup (page 140) to make you never make that mistake again.

You can label your jars in numerous ways, from premade label stickers to writing directly on the glass jar with a permanent marker. My preferred method is to use tags printed at home on cardstock paper. You can design your own labels in a graphic design program, or, if you prefer, use the labels I premade for you!

With the purchase of *Gifts in Jars*, you have access to free, printable, custom labels and tags for every single gift jar in this book. **Every one!**

DOWNLOAD THE TAGS FOR EVERY GIFT FOR FREE AT THIS WEBSITE
zestmedia.co/giftsinjars

How to Download and Print the Tags

On the website shown above, you'll be able to download the tag for each gift in a PDF format to your computer. Once downloaded to your computer, you can then use a PDF viewer (like Acrobat Reader) to print the files. No special settings are required.

BUILDING OUT YOUR GIFTS

Whether it's a milestone birthday or celebrating a teacher who went the extra mile, sometimes you want to give a gift that has a little more oomph! In those cases, you can let your jar be the center of a larger gift and build out from there. Here are a few example ideas to get you started.

Chili Night Gift Basket

Combine the Three-Bean Chili Mix (page 124) with the canned goods needed to make the recipe, some new bowls and spoons, and a nice tea towel.

Cookie Mix Gifts

Tie up one of the cookie mixes (starting page 26) with the tools to help accomplish the job! Cookie cutters, wooden spoons, rubber spatulas, and silicone baking mats are all great options.

Movie Night Gift Basket

Combine the Popcorn Seasonings (page 40) with microwave popcorn, movie theatre candy boxes, and a movie rental gift card.

Pizza Night Gift Basket

Combine the Garlic and Herb Pizza Crust (page 130) with Sun-Dried Tomatoes (page 104) and some other pizza fixings—like pepperoni, Parmesan, pizza sauce, and a cutter.

baking mixes

Baking at home is a beautiful family activity, and these baking mixes in a jar are the perfect way to give that fun! Each jar is filled with pre-measured ingredients that come together effortlessly to create delicious treats in no time.

BROWNIE MIX

CRANBERRY ORANGE MUFFIN MIX

DOUBLE CHOCOLATE MUFFIN MIX

CONFETTI CAKE MIX

GINGERBREAD COOKIE MIX

M&M COOKIE MIX

SNICKERDOODLE COOKIE MIX

GLUTEN-FREE CHOCOLATE CHIP COOKIE MIX

WHOLE GRAIN PANCAKE MIX

GLUTEN-FREE PANCAKE MIX

HANDMADE WITH

RICH AND FUDGY
Brownies

INSTRUCTIONS: Preheat oven to 350°F. Line a 9" x 9" pan with parchment paper or aluminum foil, spray liberally with cooking spray. Set aside. In a medium mixing bowl, combine 2 cups of the brownie mix with 1/2 cup melted butter or oil, 2 eggs, and 1 teaspoon vanilla extract. Stir until well combined. Spread into the prepared pan and bake in a preheated oven for 20-25 minutes, or until a toothpick inserted about an inch away from the edge of the pan comes out mostly clean. Let cool completely before removing from pan and slicing into squares.

brownie mix

Gift the gift of rich, fudgy brownies with this easy-to-assemble brownie mix. I like adding chocolate chips or chopped walnuts to the mix but feel free to experiment with other mix-ins. I think peanut butter chips would be delicious!

INGREDIENTS
for the mix
- 2 cups granulated sugar
- 1 cup unsweetened cocoa powder
- 1 cup all-purpose flour
- 1/2 teaspoon salt
- 1 cup chocolate chips or chopped walnuts, optional

for the brownies
- 1/2 cup melted butter or vegetable oil
- 2 eggs
- 1 teaspoon vanilla extract

DIRECTIONS
to make the mix jars
1. Mix all ingredients in a large bowl, whisking to combine thoroughly.
2. Transfer mix to a quart-sized mason jar and close lid.
3. Decorate the jar as desired (see page 11 for ideas) and tie on the tag.

to bake the brownies
1. Preheat oven to 350°F. Line a 9" x 9" pan with parchment paper or aluminum foil, and spray liberally with cooking spray. Set aside.
2. In a medium mixing bowl, combine 2 cups of the brownie mix with the melted butter or oil, egg, and vanilla. Stir until well combined.
3. Spread into the prepared pan and bake in a preheated oven for 20-25 minutes, or until a toothpick inserted about an inch away from the edge of the pan comes out mostly clean.
4. Let cool completely before removing from the pan and slicing into squares.

Cranberry Orange MUFFIN MIX

HANDMADE WITH ♥

Combine the muffin mix with 1 beaten egg, 1 cup of orange juice, and 1/4 cup melted butter or vegetable oil. Fill cups of a greased muffin tin 3/4 full with the mixture. Bake in a 425°F oven for 5 minutes, then reduce heat to 350°F and bake for an additional 12-15 minutes, or until a toothpick inserted in the middle of a muffin comes out clean.

cranberry orange muffin mix

Who doesn't love fluffy, delicious muffins? These are spiked with tangy cranberries and orange zest. If you've never bought dried orange peel, you can usually find it in the herbs and spices section of most major supermarkets.

INGREDIENTS
for the mix
- 2 cups all-purpose flour
- 1/2 cup sugar
- 4 teaspoons baking powder
- 1/4 teaspoon salt
- 1/2 teaspoon ground cinnamon
- 1 cup dried cranberries
- 1 tablespoon dried orange zest

for the muffins
- 1 large egg, beaten
- 1 cup orange juice
- 1/4 cup melted butter or vegetable oil

DIRECTIONS
to make the mix jars
1. Layer all ingredients in the order listed in a quart-size wide-mouth mason jar.
2. Decorate the jar as desired (see page 11 for ideas) and tie on the tag.

to bake the muffins
1. Preheat oven to 425°F. Line the cups of a muffin tin with liners, then spray liberally with cooking spray and set aside.
2. Combine the mix with the egg, orange juice, and melted butter or vegetable oil until mostly combined (a few lumps left are fine).
3. Scoop mix into prepared muffin tin, filling the cups about 3/4 of the way full.
4. Bake in the preheated oven for 5 minutes, then reduce heat to 350°F and bake for an additional 12-15 minutes, or until a toothpick inserted in the middle of a muffin comes out clean.

HANDMADE WITH ♥

Double Chocolate
MUFFIN MIX

Preheat oven to 425°F. Line the cups of muffin tin with liners. Combine the mix with 1 egg, 1/4 cup melted butter or vegetable oil, 3/4 cup sour cream, 1 1/2 teaspoons vanilla extract and 1/2 cup milk until combined (a few lumps left is fine). Scoop mix into prepared muffin tin, filling the cups about 3/4 way full. Bake in the preheated oven for 5 minutes, then reduce heat to 350° and bake an additional 12-15 minutes, or until a toothpick inserted in the middle of the muffins comes out clean.

double chocolate muffin mix

This gift is for all the chocolate lovers on your list! Rich dark chocolate muffins are studded with semi-sweet chocolate chips to make a to-die-for chocolate breakfast pastry.

INGREDIENTS
for the mix
- 1 cup all-purpose flour
- 1 1/4 teaspoon baking powder
- 1/4 teaspoon baking soda
- 1/4 teaspoon salt
- 1/2 cup unsweetened cocoa powder
- 2/3 cup granulated sugar
- 1 cup semi-sweet chocolate chips

for the muffins
- 1 large egg, beaten
- 3/4 cup sour cream
- 1/2 cup milk
- 1/4 cup melted butter or vegetable oil
- 1 1/2 teaspoons vanilla extract

DIRECTIONS
to make the mix jars
1. Layer all ingredients in the order listed in a quart-size wide-mouth mason jar.
2. Decorate the jar as desired (see page 11 for ideas) and tie on the tag.

to bake the muffins
1. Preheat oven to 425°F. Line the cups of a muffin tin with liners, then spray liberally with cooking spray and set aside.
2. Combine the mix with egg, sour cream, milk, melted butter or vegetable oil, and vanilla extract until mostly combined (a few lumps left are fine).
3. Scoop mix into prepared muffin tin, dividing the batter evenly between the 12 cups (filling the cups about 3/4 of the way full each.)
4. Bake in the preheated oven for 5 minutes, then reduce heat to 350°F and bake an additional 12-15 minutes, or until a toothpick inserted in the middle of the muffins comes out clean.

HANDMADE WITH

Confetti Cake Mix

- Preheat oven to 350°F. Line a 9"x9" pan with parchment, spray with cooking spray.
- In a medium mixing bowl, combine mix, 1/2 cup softened butter, 3 egg whites, 2 teaspoons vanilla extract, and 1 cup water and beat on medium speed for 2 minutes or until light and fluffy.
- Spread into the prepared pan and bake in a preheated oven for 25-30 minutes, or until a toothpick inserted in the middle of the pan comes out clean.
- Let cool completely, then frost and decorate with additional sprinkles.

confetti cake mix

Who doesn't love a good confetti cake? This vanilla cake is dotted with colorful sprinkles and is a perfect treat for a birthday or any celebration. The key ingredient to making this cake mix full of flavor is powdered buttermilk. You'll find it in the baking section of most major supermarkets.

INGREDIENTS

for the mix

- 2 cups all-purpose flour
- 3 tablespoons cornstarch
- 3 tablespoons powdered buttermilk (available in the baking section of most supermarkets)
- 2/3 cup sprinkles
- 1 cup granulated sugar
- 1 1/2 teaspoons baking powder
- 1/2 teaspoon baking soda
- 1/2 teaspoon salt

for the cake

- 1/2 cup (1 stick) unsalted butter, softened to room temperature
- 3 large egg whites
- 1 cup water
- 2 teaspoons pure vanilla extract
- Vanilla frosting
- Additional sprinkles for decorating

protip

The best sprinkles I've found for both color and texture are jimmies or the small round wafer confetti sprinkles. Naturally colored sprinkles don't tend to hold their bright color in the oven as well as artificially colored sprinkles.

DIRECTIONS

to make the mix jars

1. Layer all ingredients in the order listed in a quart-size wide-mouth mason jar.
2. Decorate the jar as desired (see page 11 for ideas) and tie on the tag.

to bake the cake

1. Preheat oven to 350°F. Line a 9" x 9" pan with parchment paper and spray liberally with cooking spray. Set aside.
2. In a medium mixing bowl, combine the cake mix, butter, egg whites, water, and vanilla, and beat on medium speed for 2 minutes, or until light and fluffy.
3. Spread into the prepared pan and bake in a preheated oven for 25-30 minutes, or until a toothpick inserted in the middle of the pan comes out clean.
4. Let cool completely, then frost and decorate with additional sprinkles.

On the gift tag:

CLASSIC ★ DELICIOUS
Gingerbread Cookies

makes 2 dozen cookies

YOU'LL NEED:
2/3 cup butter, softened
1 large egg
1 teaspoon vanilla extract
2/3 cup molasses
1 jar of cookie mix

TO MAKE:
Using an electric mixer, combine the butter, egg, molasses, and vanilla. Add in the jar of cookie mix and mix on low until combined. The dough will be quite thick. Divide the dough in half, and wrap each half in plastic wrap and form into a disc. Chill for at least 2 hours. After chill time, preheat oven to 350°F. Line a baking sheet with parchment or a silicone baking mat. Remove one disc of dough from the fridge and let warm on the counter for 10 minutes, then unwrap, and roll on a floured surface until 1/4-inch thick. Cut out cookies using cookie cutters, and place 1-inch apart on the prepared baking sheet. Bake for 7-10 minutes depending on the size of the cookie. Let cool for 5 minutes on the baking sheet, then transfer to a baking rack to cool completely before decorating.

MAKES 1 QUART JAR MIX
each quart jar makes 2 dozen cookies

gingerbread cookie mix

Soft, spiced, and sweet, this gingerbread cookie mix makes the most delectable holiday cookies around! These cookies roll out to make perfect gingerbread men.

INGREDIENTS

for the mix

- 3 1/2 cups (435g) all-purpose flour, divided in half
- 1 teaspoon baking soda
- 1/2 teaspoon salt
- 3/4 cup (150g) packed dark brown sugar
- 1 tablespoon ground ginger
- 1 tablespoon ground cinnamon
- 1/2 teaspoon ground allspice
- 1/2 teaspoon ground cloves
- 1/4 teaspoon finely ground black pepper, optional

for the cookies

- 2/3 cup butter, softened
- 1 large egg, beaten
- 2/3 cup molasses
- 1 teaspoon vanilla extract

26

DIRECTIONS

to make the mix jars

1. In a quart-size wide-mouth mason jar, layer half of the flour followed by all remaining ingredients, then finish with the remaining half of the flour. Close the lid.
2. Decorate the jar as desired (see page 11 for ideas) and tie on the tag.

to bake the cookies

1. Use an electric mixer to combine the butter, egg, molasses, and vanilla in a medium bowl.
2. Add the cookie mix, and stir on low until combined. The dough will be quite thick.
3. Divide the dough in half. Wrap each half in plastic wrap and form into a disc. Chill for at least 2 hours.
4. After chill time, preheat oven to 350°F. Line a baking sheet with parchment or a silicone baking mat.
5. Remove one disc of the dough from the fridge and let it warm on the counter for 10 minutes. Keep the other disc chilled until you are ready to use it.
6. Unwrap and roll out the dough on a floured surface until 1/4-inch thick. Cut out cookies using cookie cutters, and place 1" apart on the prepared baking sheet. Gather scraps, reroll, and cut more cookies.
7. Bake for 7-10 minutes, depending on size. Let cool for 5 minutes on the baking sheet, then transfer to a baking rack to cool completely before decorating. Repeat with remaining chilled dough disc.

protip

You can tie a metal cookie cutter to these jars to make them even more festive!

DOWNLOAD THE TAGS FOR THIS GIFT FOR FREE
zestmedia.co/giftsinjars

6

M&M Cookies

COMBINE MIX IN A BOWL WITH:

1 BEATEN
Egg

1/2 CUP (1 STICK)
Melted Butter

2 TEASPOONS
Van...

Roll into 1 1/2" balls. Place 2" apart on a cookie sheet lined with parchment or a baking mat. Bake at 350°F for 8 to 10 minutes. Let cool for 5 minutes, then transfer to wire rack to cool completely.

MAKES 2 DOZEN

m+m cookie mix

Give the gift of holiday baking! These M&M Cookies are chewy, tender, and perfectly festive! Feel free to use different colored M&Ms for other celebrations.

INGREDIENTS
for the mix
- 1/4 cup granulated sugar
- 1 1/4 cups all-purpose flour
- 1 teaspoon baking powder
- 1/2 teaspoon baking soda
- 1/2 teaspoon sea salt
- 1/2 cup rolled oats
- 1 cup M&M Minis/Baking Bits or regular M&Ms
- 1/2 cup packed brown sugar

for the cookies
- 1/2 cup (1 stick) butter, melted
- 1 large egg, beaten
- 2 teaspoons vanilla extract

DIRECTIONS
to make the mix jars
1. Layer all ingredients in the order listed in a quart-size wide-mouth mason jar.
2. Decorate the jar as desired (see page 11 for ideas) and tie on the tag.

to bake the cookies
1. Preheat oven to 350°F. Line a baking sheet with parchment paper or a silicone baking mat. Set aside.
2. In a medium mixing bowl, combine the cookie mix with the melted butter, egg, and vanilla. Stir until well combined.
3. Roll dough into 1 1/2" balls, and place on the prepared baking sheet 2" apart. Bake in preheated oven for 8-10 minutes, or until slightly brown along the edges but still very soft in the middle.
4. Let cool for 5 minutes on the baking sheet, then transfer to a wire rack to cool completely.

HANDMADE WITH ♥
Snickerdoodles
makes 2 dozen cookies

YOU'LL NEED:
- 3/4 cup softened butter
- 2 eggs
- 1 teaspoon vanilla
- 2 tablespoons sugar
- 1 tablespoon cinnamon

TO MAKE:
1. Preheat oven to 400°F. Line a baking sheet with parchment paper or a silicone baking mat.
2. In a medium mixing bowl, beat the butter, eggs, and vanilla until smooth. Add in the cookie mix and stir until well combined.
3. Combine the sugar and cinnamon in a small bowl. Then roll the dough into 1 1/2" balls, roll balls into the cinnamon sugar mixture to coat.
4. Place on the prepared baking sheet 2" apart. Bake in preheated oven for 8-10 minutes, or until slightly brown along the edges but still very soft in the middle.
5. Let cool for 5 minutes on the baking sheet, then transfer to a wire rack to cool completely.

snickerdoodle cookie mix

A good snickerdoodle cookie is soft and tender and sparkling with cinnamon sugar. The secret ingredient to getting that classic snickerdoodle flavor is cream of tartar! This ingredient adds a bit of tang to the dough that balances the sweetness perfectly.

INGREDIENTS

for the mix

- 1 cup sugar
- 1/2 cup packed brown sugar
- 2 3/4 cups all-purpose flour
- 1 teaspoon cream of tartar
- 1/2 teaspoon baking soda
- 1/4 teaspoon salt

for the cookies

- 3/4 cup softened butter
- 2 large eggs
- 1 teaspoon vanilla extract
- 2 tablespoons granulated sugar
- 1 tablespoon cinnamon

protip

Package this jar in a gift basket with a jar of Cinnamon Sugar (page 108) to save your recipient a step!

DIRECTIONS

to make the mix jars

1. Layer all ingredients in the order listed in a quart-size wide-mouth mason jar.
2. Decorate the jar as desired (see page 11 for ideas) and tie on the tag.

to bake the cookies

1. Preheat oven to 400°F. Line a baking sheet with parchment paper or a silicone baking mat. Set aside.
2. In a medium mixing bowl, beat the butter, eggs, and vanilla until smooth. Add in the cookie mix and stir until well combined.
3. Combine the sugar and cinnamon in a small bowl. Roll the dough into 1 1/2" balls, and roll the balls in the cinnamon sugar mixture to coat.
4. Place dough balls on the prepared baking sheet 2" apart. Bake in preheated oven for 8-10 minutes, or until slightly brown along the edges but still very soft in the middle.
5. Let cool for 5 minutes on the baking sheet, then transfer to a wire rack to cool completely.

gluten-free chocolate chip cookie mix

These gluten-free chocolate chip cookies come out soft and tender with the perfect amount of rich chocolate chips! Gift this jar to a loved one who avoids gluten but still loves the sweeter things in life.

INGREDIENTS

for the mix

- 1 1/2 cup gluten-free all-purpose flour, see protip
- 1/2 teaspoon baking soda
- 1/2 teaspoon salt
- 1 cup semi-sweet chocolate chips
- 1/2 cup chopped walnuts or pecans, optional
- 1/4 cup granulated sugar
- 1/2 cup packed brown sugar

for the cookies

- 3/4 cup (1 1/2 sticks) melted butter
- 1 large egg
- 1 large egg yolk
- 1 teaspoon vanilla extract

protip

Gluten-free flours vary widely, but we've found this recipe to be pretty forgiving to different flour brands. This was tested using Better Batter Original All-Purpose Flour Blend.

DIRECTIONS

to make the mix jars

1. Layer all ingredients in the order listed in a quart-size wide-mouth mason jar.
2. Decorate the jar as desired (see page 11 for ideas) and tie on the tag.

to bake the cookies

1. Line a baking sheet with parchment paper or a silicone baking mat. Set aside.
2. In a medium mixing bowl, combine all of the cookie mix with the melted butter, egg, egg yolk, and vanilla. Stir until well combined. The dough will be soft and greasy.
3. Chill dough for 20 minutes. At the end of the chill time, preheat oven to 350°F.
4. Roll into 1 1/2" balls, and place on the prepared baking sheet 2" apart.
5. Bake cookies in preheated oven for 10-12 minutes, or until slightly brown along the edges but still very soft in the middle.
6. Let cool for 10 minutes on the baking sheet, then transfer to a wire rack to cool completely.

whole grain pancake mix

This whole grain pancake mix makes fluffy, tender pancakes packed with fiber and the irresistible nutty flavor of whole grains. The two secret ingredients here? Chopped up whole oats, which add an amazing chew, and white whole wheat flour—a whole grain flour that has the nutty flavor of whole wheat with the fluffy texture of white flour!

INGREDIENTS

for the mix

- 3 1/2 cups old-fashioned oats
- 4 cups white whole wheat flour
- 1 cup all-purpose flour
- 3 tablespoons granulated sugar
- 3 tablespoons baking powder
- 1 tablespoon baking soda
- 1 tablespoon sea salt
- 1 cup vegetable oil (or avocado oil)

for the pancakes

- 1 cup packed pancake mix
- 1 cup buttermilk
- 1 large egg

protip

This will store for about a month at room temperature, but for longer storage, keep it in the freezer for up to three months.

DIRECTIONS

to make the mix jars

1. Grind the oats in a food processor until finely chopped, but not completely powdered. Pour the oats into the bowl of a stand mixer fitted with the paddle attachment.
2. Add the white whole wheat flour, all-purpose flour, sugar, baking powder, baking soda, and salt. Mix on low until thoroughly combined.
3. With the mixer still on low, pour in the oil slowly and continue to mix until well incorporated.
4. Transfer the mix to a half-gallon jar. Decorate the jar as desired (see page 11 for ideas) and add the tag.

to make pancakes

1. Whisk together pancake mix, buttermilk, and egg. Let the batter rest for 15-20 minutes (the oats will absorb some of the liquid).
2. Heat a cast iron skillet or griddle over medium heat. When hot, add enough butter or oil to coat the bottom of the pan. Add about 1/4 cup of batter to the hot pan. Cook for 2-3 minutes, until bubbles appear on the top and the outer edges of the pancake begin to look dry. Flip and cook for 1-2 minutes on the second side.
3. Repeat for the remaining batter, adding more butter to the pan whenever it looks dry. Serve pancakes hot with desired toppings.

GLUTEN FREE
Pancake Mix

TO MAKE PANCAKES: Combine 1 cup of
mix with 1 cup of milk, 1 large egg,
2 tablespoons melted butter or oil, and
1 teaspoon of vanilla extract

One batch makes 6 to 8, 4" pancakes

MAKES 1 QUART MIX

each quart jar makes 3 batches pancakes

gluten-free pancake mix

Have someone on your list who avoids gluten? They'll be so happy to receive this pancake mix! This mix makes pancakes that are free-from-gluten, but just as fluffy and tender as regular pancakes.

INGREDIENTS

for the mix

- 3 cups all-purpose gluten-free flour
- 1/3 cup granulated sugar
- 2 tablespoons gluten-free baking powder
- 1/2 teaspoon salt

for the pancakes

- 1 cup mix
- 1 cup milk
- 1 large egg
- 2 tablespoons melted butter or vegetable oil
- 1 teaspoon vanilla extract

DIRECTIONS

to make the mix jars

1. Whisk all ingredients together in a large bowl, and transfer to a quart-sized mason jar.
2. Decorate the jar as desired (see page 11 for ideas) and tie on the tag.

to make pancakes

1. Combine mix, milk, egg, butter or vegetable oil, and vanilla extract in a medium-sized bowl, and whisk together until smooth. Let rest for 5-10 minutes.
2. While the batter rests, preheat a large skillet or griddle over medium-low heat, then spray with nonstick spray or brush with melted butter. Scoop 1/4 cup batter onto the hot surface. Then, when lots of bubbles form on the top and sides of the pancakes and pop, and the bottom of the pancake is golden brown, flip the pancake and cook until the second side of the pancake is golden brown.

HANDMADE WITH ♥

Nuts

salty snacks

Give the gift of savory snacks! So often folks get sweets when given handmade food gifts, but you can flip the script with these salty options. Or even better, pair one salty snack jar with one sweet snack jar for the ultimate snack bundle!

POPCORN SEASONINGS

ROSEMARY PARTY NUTS

SWEET AND SPICY MIXED NUTS

TRAIL MIXES

CHEESE STRAWS

ROASTED CHICKPEAS

NUTS 'N' BOLTS

popcorn seasonings

Everyone's favorite movie snack gets even better with gourmet popcorn seasoning! Just sprinkle these seasonings onto freshly-popped popcorn for an explosion of flavor.

INGREDIENTS

ranch popcorn seasoning

- 2 to 4 tablespoons fine sea salt, to taste
- 2 tablespoons onion powder
- 2 tablespoons dried parsley
- 2 tablespoons garlic powder
- 2 tablespoons dried dill
- 1 tablespoon dry mustard
- 1 tablespoon celery seed
- 2 teaspoons paprika
- 1 to 3 teaspoons black pepper, to taste

dill pickle popcorn seasoning

- 1/4 cup dried dill
- 2 to 4 tablespoons fine sea salt, to taste, omit if using microwave popcorn
- 2 to 4 tablespoons white vinegar powder, to taste, optional but recommended (available online and at some supermarkets)
- 2 tablespoons ground turmeric
- 2 tablespoons ground coriander
- 2 tablespoons garlic powder

cinnamon sugar popcorn seasoning

- 1/2 cup granulated sugar
- 1/3 cup ground cinnamon
- 1 to 2 tablespoons fine sea salt, to taste, omit if using microwave popcorn
- 1 teaspoon vanilla bean powder, optional

DIRECTIONS

1. Add all ingredients for your chosen seasoning to a small bowl and whisk until well combined.
2. Transfer to a half-pint size mason jar. Decorate the jar as desired (see page 11 for ideas) and tie on the tag.

protips

Pop these jars in a basket with some microwave popcorn and some movie theatre candy boxes for a cute family gift.

These seasonings will stick the best on buttered popcorn, but you can also get the seasoning to stick to air-popped popcorn by using a coffee grinder to grind the seasoning into a very fine powder.

Rosemary
Party Nuts

100% HANDMADE · MADE WITH LOVE

rosemary party nuts

These addictive mixed nuts are packed with savory rosemary flavor! I like pairing a jar of these salty nuts with a jar of something sweet for a wonderfully balanced gift.

INGREDIENTS

- 2 cups raw cashews
- 2 cups raw almonds
- 1 cup raw walnut halves
- 1 cup raw pecan halves
- 1 cup unsalted shelled pistachios
- 1 cup unsalted roasted peanuts
- 1 stick (8 tablespoons) unsalted butter, melted
- 1/2 cup chopped fresh rosemary
- 2 tablespoons Worcestershire sauce
- 2 tablespoons chopped fresh thyme
- 1 tablespoon sea salt
- 1 teaspoon garlic powder
- 1 teaspoon onion powder

DIRECTIONS

1. Preheat oven to 250°F. Line a large, rimmed baking sheet with parchment paper.
2. Add nuts to a large bowl and mix well to combine.
3. In a small bowl, whisk together the melted butter, rosemary, Worcestershire sauce, thyme, sea salt, garlic powder, and onion powder. Pour over top of the nuts, and then toss to coat the nuts.
4. Bake nuts for about an hour, stirring well with a spatula every 15 minutes. Nuts are ready when they begin to brown and most of the liquid has been absorbed.
5. Remove from oven and allow to cool completely on the pan before dividing into two quart-size canning jars. Nuts will be soft while still warm.
6. Decorate the jars as desired (see page 11 for ideas) and tie on the tags.

sweet and spicy mixed nuts

These mixed nuts have a hint of sweetness thanks to maple syrup and brown sugar, and a little bit of a kick thanks to some chili powder! I find the combo to be irresistible. I like to keep these on hand for parties and gatherings, and they are always a hit!

INGREDIENTS

- 2 cups raw cashews
- 2 cups raw almonds
- 1 1/2 cups raw walnut halves
- 1 1/2 cups raw pecan halves
- 1/4 cup (1/2 a stick) melted butter
- 3 tablespoons maple syrup
- 3 tablespoons brown sugar
- 2 teaspoons fine sea salt
- 1 teaspoon chili powder
- 1/2 to 1 teaspoon cayenne pepper, to taste

DIRECTIONS

1. Preheat oven to 250°F. Line a large, rimmed baking sheet with parchment paper.
2. Add nuts to a large bowl and mix well to combine.
3. In a small bowl, whisk together the melted butter, maple syrup, brown sugar, salt, chili powder, and cayenne pepper. Pour over top of the nuts, and then toss to coat the nuts.
4. Bake nuts for about an hour, stirring well with a spatula every 15 minutes. Nuts are ready when they are starting to brown and most of the liquid has been absorbed.
5. Remove from oven and allow to cool completely on the pan before dividing into two quart-size canning jars. Nuts will be soft while still warm.
6. Decorate the jars as desired (see page 11 for ideas) and tie on the tags.

trail mixes

Homemade trail mix couldn't be easier to make (we're talking a minute or two total time!), and it's always a well-loved gift. I like giving these jars to the hikers, anglers, and other outdoorsy folks on my list.

INGREDIENTS

peanut butter lovers' trail mix

- 1/2 cup mini peanut butter cups
- 1/2 cup Reese's pieces
- 1 cup peanuts
- 1 cup raisins
- 1/2 cup peanut butter chips
- 1/2 cup chocolate chips
- 1 cup mini pretzels

cranberry and pistachio trail mix

- 1 cup dried cranberries
- 1 cup shelled pistachios
- 1 cup white chocolate chips
- 1 cup almonds

classic trail mix

- 1 cup M&Ms
- 1 cup peanuts
- 1 cup raisins
- 1 cup cashews

DIRECTIONS

1. Combine the ingredients for each trail mix in a medium bowl. Stir well to mix.
2. Transfer to a wide-mouth quart jar. Decorate the jar as desired (see page 11 for ideas) and add the label.

protip

It's really hard to mess up homemade trail mix, so feel free to come up with your own perfect mix! I like to stick with a combo of something sweet, something salty, and something fruity—but let your imagination take over!

CRUNCHY & SAVORY

Cheese Straws

A GREAT ADDITION TO CHARCUTERIE BOARDS!

HANDMADE WITH LOVE

cheese straws

Savory cheese straws are crispy, buttery, and packed with sharp cheddar flavor. You can form your cheese straws in multiple ways—pipe them, cut them with a knife or pizza cutter, or use a cookie press.

INGREDIENTS

- 8 ounces extra sharp cheddar cheese, shredded
- 3/4 cup (1 1/2 sticks) unsalted butter
- 1 egg
- 1 teaspoon hot sauce
- 1 3/4 cups all-purpose flour
- 1/2 teaspoon paprika
- 1 teaspoon dry mustard
- 1/2 teaspoon salt

protip

For the best texture and flavor, make sure to shred your own cheese off the block instead of using pre-shredded cheese in a bag.

DIRECTIONS

1. Preheat oven to 400°F.
2. In the basin of a food processor, pulse together the cheese, butter, egg, and hot sauce until light and fluffy.
3. In a small mixing bowl, whisk together the flour, paprika, dry mustard, and salt. Add the dry ingredients to the food processor in two additions, pulsing to combine after each. Continue pulsing until the dough comes together and forms a ball.

if piping the straws or using a cookie press

1. Fit a cookie press with the desired die or a piping bag with a large piping tip. Fill with half of the dough.
2. Pipe or press long straws of the dough onto an ungreased baking sheet. Repeat with remaining dough. You may need more than one baking sheet.
3. Using a sharp knife, cut the long straws into 6-inch pieces. Bake in preheated oven for 5-7 minutes, or until the straws are golden brown. Let cool for 3-5 minutes on the baking sheet, then transfer to a wire rack to cool completely.
4. Place straws in a jar (you might need to break some to get them to fit). Decorate the jar as desired (see page 11 for ideas) and tie on the tag.

if rolling out the dough

1. Divide the dough into two discs, wrap each in plastic wrap, and chill for 30 minutes. Remove one disc from the fridge, and roll out on a piece of parchment paper until 1/4" thick.
2. Using a sharp knife or a pizza cutter, cut into long thin strips. Transfer the parchment paper to a baking sheet. Repeat with remaining dough on a second baking sheet.
3. Bake in preheated oven for 5-7 minutes, or until the straws are golden brown. Let cool for 3-5 minutes, then transfer to a wire rack to cool completely.
4. Place straws in a jar (you might need to break some to get them to fit). Decorate the jar as desired (see page 11 for ideas) and tie on the tag.

HANDMADE WITH

CRUNCHY

Roasted
Chickpeas

roasted chickpeas

Did you know that chickpeas get delightfully crunchy when you pop them in the oven for a bit? These crunchy, crispy chickpeas make an awesome protein-packed snack for anyone on your list.

INGREDIENTS

- 4 1/2 cups cooked chickpeas (3 cans worth, drained, rinsed, and patted dry with a clean kitchen towel)
- 4 tablespoons olive oil
- 1 teaspoon garlic powder
- 1 teaspoon smoked paprika
- 1 teaspoon sea salt
- 1/2 teaspoon black pepper
- 1/2 teaspoon ground cayenne pepper

DIRECTIONS

1. Preheat oven to 425°F. Cover a large baking sheet with parchment paper and set aside.
2. In a large zip-top bag or bowl, whisk together the olive oil, garlic powder, smoked paprika, salt, pepper, and cayenne. Add the chickpeas, close the zip top, and shake until all the chickpeas are coated.
3. Pour the chickpeas out onto the prepared baking sheet. Roast in preheated oven for 50-60 minutes, stirring every 10 minutes, or until crunchy and browned.
4. Immediately after removing from oven, taste for seasoning, adding more salt if desired.
5. Allow to cool completely on the baking sheet before transferring to a pint-size canning jar.
6. Decorate the jar as desired (see page 11 for ideas) and tie on the tag.

MAKES 2 HALF-GALLON JARS

nuts 'n' bolts

This snack mix is a beloved family recipe passed down from my mother-in-law. I make it by the gallon each Christmas, and it's so popular with my friends and family that I think I'd be disowned if I skipped making it one year!

INGREDIENTS

- 2 cups Cheerios cereal
- 2 cups Corn Chex cereal
- 2 cups Rice Chex cereal
- 2 cups cheese crackers (like Goldfish or Cheez-Its)
- 1 cup mini pretzels twists or rods
- 1 cup smoked almonds
- 1 cup roasted peanuts
- 1 cup cashews

- 1/2 cup butter
- 1 tablespoon Worcestershire sauce
- 2 teaspoons garlic powder
- 2 teaspoons onion powder
- 2 teaspoons smoked paprika
- 1 teaspoon seasoned salt (like Lawry's)
- 2 cups potato sticks

DIRECTIONS

1. Preheat oven to 250°F. Line two large, rimmed baking sheets with parchment paper and set aside.
2. In a very large mixing bowl, combine the Cheerios, Corn Chex, Rice Chex, cheese crackers, pretzels, almonds, peanuts, and cashews. Stir to combine and set aside.
3. In a small saucepan, combine the butter, Worcestershire sauce, garlic powder, onion powder, smoked paprika, and seasoned salt. Heat over medium-low heat until the butter is melted.
4. Whisk the butter mixture well, then pour over the cereal mixture. Stir the cereal mix to coat every piece.
5. Divide the mixture between the two baking sheets and spread out into an even layer on each.
6. Bake in preheated oven for 90 minutes, stirring the mix every 30 minutes.
7. When the mix comes out of the oven, stir in the potato sticks.
8. Once the mix is cool, transfer it into two half-gallon jars and close the lids. Decorate the jars as desired (see page 11 for ideas) and tie on the tags.

protip

It's easy to make this mix gluten-free! Just make sure to grab gluten-free cereals, pretzels, and cheese crackers, and you're good to go.

DOWNLOAD THE TAGS FOR THIS GIFT FOR FREE
zestmedia.co/giftsinjars

TURTLES • PAGE 68

sweet snacks

Nothing says, "I'm thinking of you" quite like the gift of a sweet treat. Sharing a delicious homemade sweet is somehow so heartfelt.

SEA SALT HONEY CARAMELS

PEPPERMINT BARK

EDIBLE COOKIE DOUGH

CRANBERRY PISTACHIO BARK

PEANUT BUTTER CHOCOLATE CHIP GRANOLA

BUCKEYES

TURTLES

PUPPY CHOW

SOFT & RICH

Honey
Caramels

sea salt honey caramels

Homemade caramels might sound intimidating, but I promise they're a breeze to make and incredibly impressive to gift! I make a batch of these sea salt honey caramels every holiday season to give away—always to rave reviews.

INGREDIENTS

- 1 1/2 cups sugar
- 1/2 cup honey
- 1 stick unsalted butter, softened and cut into large chunks
- 1 cup heavy cream
- 1 teaspoon coarse sea salt

DIRECTIONS

1. Line a 9" x 13" baking dish or 9" x 9" baking dish (which will make thicker, but fewer, caramels) with wax or parchment paper, leaving long overhangs on two sides. Spray paper with cooking spray and set aside.
2. In a large saucepan, combine sugar and honey. Heat over medium heat until smooth and melted. Bring to a boil, reduce heat, and simmer until sugar has darkened to a deep caramel color—about 5 minutes. Watch carefully, as sugar burns fast!
3. Reduce the heat to low and whisk in the knobs of butter one at a time. Be prepared, the mixture will bubble and grow (hence the large pot). Once all the butter is mixed in, whisk in the cream.
4. Bring the pot to a boil over medium heat and continue to boil until the mixture reaches the hard ball stage (about 244°F on a thermometer or when you drop some of the caramel in cold water, you can form it into a hardish ball). Remove from heat and pour caramel into the prepared pan.
5. Place the pan in the fridge for about 10 minutes to set up slightly, then sprinkle the top of the caramels with sea salt. Let caramels set up at room temperature for about an hour, or until totally cooled.
6. To remove, gently pull on the paper overhang and remove the caramel block from the baking sheet. Cut into squares with a sharp knife and wrap in small pieces of wax paper.
7. Place wrapped caramels in a jar. Decorate the jar as desired (see page 11 for ideas) and tie on the tag.

HANDCRAFTED
Peppermint Bark

peppermint bark

A classic for a reason, homemade peppermint bark is incredibly easy to make, super delicious, and the perfect gift for neighbors, coworkers, teachers, or mail carriers around the holidays.

INGREDIENTS

- 8 peppermint candy canes
- 12 ounces semi-sweet chocolate chips
- 12 ounces white chocolate chips

DIRECTIONS

1. Cover a large baking sheet in aluminum foil. Set aside.
2. Remove candy canes from wrapper and place in large plastic zip-top bag. Using a mallet, the bottom of a glass, or a rolling pin, mash the candy canes until they are in small chunks.
3. In a double boiler (or in a small bowl over a pot of simmering water), melt semi-sweet chocolate chips. When completely smooth, pour onto baking sheet and spread into a thin layer (about 1/8″ thick). Don't worry if the chocolate doesn't spread to the edge of the baking sheet. Place baking sheet in freezer.
4. Using a clean double boiler, melt white chocolate chips until smooth. Mix in all but 1/3 cup of the candy cane pieces.
5. Remove baking sheet from freezer and carefully spread white chocolate over the dark chocolate in a thin layer. Sprinkle 1/3 cup of reserved candy cane pieces on top. Place baking sheet in freezer.
6. Once bark is completely cooled and hard, remove from baking sheet and break into pieces.
7. Place chunks of peppermint bark in a large wide-mouth jar. Decorate the jar as desired (see page 11 for ideas) and tie on the tag.

edible cookie dough

Give the gift of the ultimate comfort snack with this edible cookie dough! This cookie dough is free from egg and raw flour, which makes it perfectly safe to consume without baking.

INGREDIENTS

- 1/2 cup tapioca flour
- 1/2 cup blanched almond flour
- 1/4 cup maple syrup
- 1/4 cup softened coconut oil or butter
- 2 teaspoons vanilla extract
- 1/4 teaspoon sea salt
- 1/3 cup mini chocolate chips or chopped dark chocolate

DIRECTIONS

1. In a small bowl, combine the tapioca flour, almond flour, maple syrup, coconut oil or grass-fed butter, vanilla, and salt. Cream together using a wooden spoon or using an electric mixer.
2. Fold in the chocolate chips or chopped dark chocolate.
3. Transfer mixture to an airtight container and store at room temperature for up to a week, in the fridge for up to a month, or in the freezer for up to six months.
4. Decorate the jars as desired (see page 11 for ideas) and tie on the tags.

protips

You can tie on a festive small spoon to the jar to make them ready-to-eat!

Bring the cookie dough to room temperature (or slightly warmer if using coconut oil) before enjoying.

DOWNLOAD THE TAGS FOR THIS GIFT FOR FREE
zestmedia.co/giftsinjars

cranberry pistachio bark

This beautiful and colorful bark is a fun sweet-tart twist on the classic peppermint bark, and is just as easy to make.

INGREDIENTS

- 7 ounces dark chocolate
- 10 ounces white chocolate
- 1/2 cup dried, sweetened cranberries
- 1/2 cup shelled, salted pistachios

DIRECTIONS

1. Line an 8″ × 8″ baking pan with parchment paper, set aside.
2. In a double boiler over medium-low heat, melt the dark chocolate, stirring constantly, until very smooth. Pour chocolate into the prepared baking pan and spread into an even layer. Let cool completely.
3. Clean out and dry the double boiler, then add the white chocolate. Melt over medium-low heat, stirring constantly until very smooth. Pour over the cooled dark chocolate and spread into an even layer.
4. Immediately sprinkle on the cranberries and pistachios. Press lightly on top to set them into the chocolate.
5. Let the bark cool completely to harden, then lift out of the pan. Break up using your hands, or cut using a sharp knife.
6. Place chunks of bark in wide-mouth jars. Decorate the jars as desired (see page 11 for ideas) and tie on the tags.

peanut butter chocolate chip granola

This Peanut Butter Chocolate Chip granola comes together in a flash and makes a big, chunky granola that is perfect for snacking.

INGREDIENTS

- 1/2 cup peanut butter (natural, unsweetened)
- 1/2 cup coconut oil
- 1/4 cup maple syrup
- 1 teaspoon vanilla extract
- 1 teaspoon salt
- 3 cups rolled oats
- 1 cup semi-sweet chocolate chips
- 1 cup roasted, unsalted peanuts

DIRECTIONS

1. Preheat the oven to 350°F. Line a baking sheet with parchment paper, set aside.
2. In a microwave-safe bowl, combine the peanut butter, coconut oil, maple syrup, vanilla, and salt. Microwave on high for 90 seconds. Stir together until smooth.
3. Pour peanut butter mixture over the oats, and stir to coat. Spread mixture in one layer onto the prepared baking sheet. Press the mixture down into the pan using the back of a wooden spoon.
4. Bake in preheated oven for 15-20 minutes, or until the granola looks golden brown. Do not overbake.
5. Let granola cool completely before stirring. Break granola up, and mix in the chocolate chips and peanuts.
6. Place granola in wide-mouth jars. Decorate the jars as desired (see page 11 for ideas) and tie on the tags.

PEANUT BUTTER
& CHOCOLATE
Buckeyes

100% HANDMADE
• MADE WITH LOVE •

buckeyes

Buckeyes are the perfect gift for the peanut butter and chocolate lover in your life! These little candies feature a soft and creamy peanut butter center dipped in rich chocolate.

INGREDIENTS

- 1 2/3 cups creamy peanut butter (not natural/unsweetened)
- 1/2 cup (1 stick) unsalted butter, softened
- 1 teaspoon vanilla extract
- 3 to 4 cups powdered sugar
- 8 ounces chopped semi-sweet chocolate or chocolate chips
- 2 tablespoons unsalted butter

protip

Buckeyes are typically larger in size (1 to 2 inches in diameter), but for packaging in jars, I recommend making them on the smaller end—closer to 1/2 inch to a full inch. Everything is cuter when it's mini anyway!

DIRECTIONS

1. Line a baking sheet with waxed paper or a silicone baking mat. Set aside.
2. Using an electric mixer, cream together the peanut butter, butter, and vanilla extract until very smooth and fluffy.
3. Add in the powdered sugar, one cup at a time, mixing well after each addition. Add as much powdered sugar as it takes for the mixture to form a non-sticky, but solid, dough—about the texture of fresh-out-of-a-new-container Play-Doh. Depending on the oil content of your peanut butter, you might need as little as 3 cups of powdered sugar, or as much as 4. Remember, you can always add more powdered sugar, but you can't take it out.
4. Using wet hands, form the dough into smooth balls no larger than 1" in diameter. Place the balls on the baking sheet. When all the balls are formed, pop the baking sheet in the freezer to set the balls while you make the chocolate coating.
5. In a double boiler on low or in a mixing bowl fitted over a small saucepan with simmering water on low heat, combine the chocolate and butter. Stir frequently until melted and smooth.
6. Remove the peanut butter balls from the freezer. Insert a wooden toothpick into the middle of one of the balls. Dip the ball in the chocolate about 2/3 of the way up the side of the ball. Return the ball to the baking sheet, dropping it off the toothpick. Repeat with the remaining peanut butter balls.
7. To close the toothpick holes, dip a finger in water and smooth over the hole. Once the chocolate is set, remove the buckeyes from the baking sheet, and store in an airtight container in the fridge.
8. Place buckeyes in jar. Decorate the jar as desired (see page 11 for ideas) and tie on the tag.

turtles

It's hard to beat a homemade turtle! These pecan and caramel candies are surprisingly easy to make using the microwave, and they are the ultimate gift for someone you know with a sweet tooth.

INGREDIENTS

- 2 cups pecan halves
- 6 tablespoons salted butter
- 1/2 cup packed brown sugar
- 1/2 cup granulated sugar
- 1/2 cup sweetened condensed milk
- 1/2 cup light corn syrup
- 1/2 teaspoon vanilla extract
- 16 oz chocolate melting wafers or high-quality chocolate

DIRECTIONS

1. Preheat oven to 350°F.
2. Spread pecans out onto a baking sheet and bake for 5-10 minutes, stirring once, until toasted and fragrant. Once cooled, roughly chop the pecans and set aside.
3. Line a baking sheet with parchment paper. Set aside.
4. Place butter in a large microwave-safe bowl and heat in microwave until melted, about 1 minute. Add brown sugar, granulated sugar, sweetened condensed milk, and corn syrup, and stir well to combine.
5. Return bowl to microwave and cook mixture on high power for about 6-8 minutes, or until it reaches about 235°F on an instant-read thermometer or passes the ice water bath test (see notes).
6. Remove the caramel from the microwave. Stir in the vanilla and chopped pecans.
7. Drop tablespoonfuls of the caramel mixture onto the parchment paper-lined baking sheet to create individual mounds of caramel candy. Refrigerate until the caramel is set, about 20 minutes.
8. Melt chocolate in microwave, stirring every 30 seconds, until melted and smooth.
9. Drop a caramel-pecan cluster into the melted chocolate and use a spoon to turn the turtle to coat the entire piece.
10. Place turtles on the parchment paper to cool. Stack turtles in wide-mouth quart jars. Decorate the jars as desired (see page 11 for ideas) and tie on the tags.

protip

To do the ice bath test: Fill a small bowl with ice water. Drop a small dollop of caramel into the ice water, and use your fingers to form the caramel into a soft ball. If it won't come together to form a ball, return it to the microwave for an additional 30 seconds, and test again.

PEANUT BUTTER & CHOCOLATE
Puppy Chow

puppy chow

Puppy Chow (AKA Muddy Buddies) is a tasty treat that's so easy to make, even kids can do it! This is my daughter's favorite kitchen craft to make for holiday gifting. Throw in some seasonal M&Ms to make it even more festive.

INGREDIENTS

- 7 cups Rice Chex Cereal
- 1 cup semi-sweet chocolate chips
- 1/2 cup creamy peanut butter
- 1/4 cup butter
- 1 teaspoon vanilla extract
- 2 cups powdered sugar

DIRECTIONS

1. Line a large baking sheet with parchment paper or waxed paper, set aside.
2. Place cereal in a large mixing bowl.
3. In a small microwave-safe bowl, combine chocolate chips, peanut butter, and butter. Heat for 1 minute, and stir to combine until completely melted. You can also do this in a double boiler over low heat on the stove.
4. Stir in the vanilla extract until smooth.
5. Pour the chocolate mixture over cereal and stir to coat.
6. In a gallon-size zip-top bag, combine powdered sugar and the cereal mixture.
7. Seal bag and toss to coat. Pour mixture onto the prepared baking sheet.
8. Allow to cool completely before transferring to quart jars. Decorate the jars as desired (see page 11 for ideas) and tie on the tags.

protip

Add seasonal M&Ms to the mix to make it more festive! I like to add 2 cups of M&Ms per batch after it has cooled.

HOT COCOA MIX • PAGE 80

drinks

From fancy liqueurs to cozy hot chocolate mix, you'll find some amazing beverage items in this chapter. These jars pair perfectly with drinkware to make a thoughtful gift, whether it be a beautiful stoneware mug or new martini glasses.

CAPPUCCINO MIX

GOLDEN MILK MIX

LOOSE LEAF CHAI

HOT COCOA MIX

COFFEE LIQUEUR

CRANBERRY LIQUEUR

LIMONCELLO

COCKTAIL KITS

IRISH CREAM

HANDMADE · WITH LOVE

Cappuccino Mix

FRENCH VANILLA

COMBINE 2 TABLESPOONS MIX WITH 8 OUNCES
BOILING WATER FOR EACH CAPPUCCINO

cappuccino mix

While this mix is far from the same as a traditional coffee shop cappuccino, it is warm, creamy, cozy, and absolutely delicious! You can change the flavor of the cappuccino by choosing different non-dairy creamer flavors.

INGREDIENTS

- 3/4 cup powdered non-dairy creamer
- 3/4 cup instant chocolate drink mix (like Nesquik)
- 3/4 cup instant espresso granules
- 1/2 cup powdered sugar

DIRECTIONS

to make the mix

1. Combine all ingredients in a large mixing bowl and whisk until well blended.
2. Scoop into a pint-size canning jar. Decorate the jar as desired (see page 11 for ideas) and tie on the tag.

to make a cappuccino

1. Combine 2 tablespoons mix with 1 cup of boiling water, and whisk until frothy.

protips

It's really important to get good-quality instant espresso or coffee granules for this recipe. I used Cafe Bustelo instant espresso in testing and loved the results!

Feel free to choose whatever non-dairy creamer flavor you'd like for your mix. Want hazelnut cappuccinos? Choose hazelnut creamer. Want French vanilla cappuccinos? Choose French vanilla creamer. You get the picture!

turmeric
GOLDEN
MILK
mix

FOR AN EARTHY, WARM,
AND COZY LATTE COMBINE
2 TABLESPOONS MIX WITH 8
OUNCES BOILING WATER

golden milk mix

Earthy and spicy, a golden milk latte is a warm and cozy drink made with turmeric, black pepper, and ginger. Some folks enjoy it for its health benefits (turmeric is a natural anti-inflammatory), and some enjoy it for its amazing taste—your giftees can enjoy it for both!

INGREDIENTS

- 2 whole vanilla beans OR 2 teaspoons vanilla bean powder
- 1 cup coconut milk powder (available at online retailers)
- 1/3 cup ground turmeric
- 2 tablespoons ground ginger
- 2 tablespoons ground cinnamon
- 1/3 cup date or coconut sugar (more or less depending on taste preference)
- 1 teaspoon ground black pepper
- 1/2 teaspoon sea salt

DIRECTIONS

to make the mix

1. If using whole vanilla beans, slice the beans in half lengthwise using a sharp knife. Scrape the vanilla flecks out of all four halves into a medium bowl. OR, if using vanilla bean powder, add that to a medium bowl.
2. Add the remaining ingredients and stir well to combine.
3. Scoop into a pint-size canning jar. Decorate the jar as desired (see page 11 for ideas) and tie on the tag.

protip

For a richer drink, combine the mix with full-fat hot coconut milk when making a latte.

to make a golden milk latte

1. Combine two heaping tablespoons of the Golden Milk Mix with 8 ounces of boiling water or hot coconut milk (for a richer drink). Whisk until frothy and smooth.
2. Sprinkle top with additional cinnamon or turmeric, if desired.

MAKES ABOUT 1 HALF-PINT TEA
enough for 12 mugs of tea

loose leaf chai

Nothing compares to the sweet and spicy flavor of masala chai! This homemade chai blend is so much more flavorful than what you get out of tea bags from the store. It also looks beautiful in the jar!

INGREDIENTS

- 12 green cardamom pods
- 1 4-inch cinnamon stick
- 1 teaspoon whole black peppercorns
- 1 teaspoon fennel seeds
- 1/2 teaspoon whole cloves
- 2 tablespoons dried cut and sifted ginger OR crystallized ginger, finely minced
- 1/2 cup loose leaf black tea, caffeinated or decaf

DIRECTIONS

to make the chai mix

1. Combine the cardamom pods, cinnamon stick, peppercorns, fennel seeds, and cloves in a mortar and pestle and roughly crush. Alternatively, place spices in a gallon zip-top bag and crush with a rolling pin.
2. Add the spice mixture to a medium skillet over medium-high heat. Toast until the spices are fragrant, about five minutes.
3. In a bowl, combine the crushed, toasted spices with the ginger and black tea.
4. Scoop into a jar. Decorate the jar as desired (see page 11 for ideas) and tie on the tag.

to make a chai latte

1. Brew the tea using a ratio of 1 1/2 tablespoons of tea mixture per 8 ounces (1 cup) of boiling water. Brew in a tea bag, tea ball, or a teapot. Steep for 7-8 minutes for caffeinated tea, and 10+ minutes for decaf tea.
2. Add 1/4 cup milk (non-dairy is fine) and natural sweetener (maple syrup, honey, or coconut sugar are all good options) to taste. Top with a sprinkle of ground cinnamon.

protip

Tie on a tea ball or other tea strainer to the jar to complete the gift.

DOWNLOAD THE TAGS FOR THIS GIFT FOR FREE
zestmedia.co/giftsinjars

WITH LOVE

HOT COCOA MIX

STIR TOGETHER 1/2 CUP OF MIX
WITH 1/2 CUP HOT WATER OR MILK

enjoy!

hot cocoa mix

My daughter and I went on a mission one winter to make the perfect hot cocoa mix that had the right flavor and silky creaminess, all while being easy enough that even a kid could make a cup. This recipe is the result, and it's so good that I get begged for the recipe every time I whip up a batch for someone new!

INGREDIENTS

- 2 cups powdered sugar
- 2 cups dried milk (whole is preferred, but nonfat works)
- 1 1/4 cups unsweetened cocoa powder (Dutch-processed preferred)
- 1 cup mini chocolate chips
- 1/4 teaspoon fine sea salt

DIRECTIONS

to make the mix

1. Stir all ingredients in a large bowl.
2. Scoop into pint-size canning jars. Decorate the jars as desired (see page 11 for ideas) and tie on the tags.

to make a mug of hot cocoa

1. Combine 1/2 cup mix with 3/4 cup of hot water or milk in a mug, and stir well until frothy and well combined.

protip

Optional but delicious add-in options for your hot cocoa mix: vanilla powder, espresso powder, mint chips, crushed candy canes, cinnamon—make it your own!

coffee liqueur

You're going to be blown away by how easy it is to make homemade coffee liqueur (AKA: Kahlúa)! My husband makes a big batch of this each holiday season, and we give away jars to all our friends and family.

INGREDIENTS

- 12 cups strong, dark brewed coffee
- 2 pounds light brown sugar
- 1/3 cup vanilla extract
- 750ml grain alcohol (like Everclear)

protip

189/190-proof grain alcohol is preferable here, but if you only get 151- or 120-proof, that will also work.

DIRECTIONS

1. Pour the coffee into a large soup pot, add in the brown sugar, and heat over medium-high heat, stirring frequently, until the sugar is dissolved, about 5 minutes.
2. Remove from the heat and let cool to room temperature.
3. Add in the vanilla and the grain alcohol. Pour into jars. Decorate the jars as desired (see page 11 for ideas) and tie on the tags.

Cranberry
Liqueur
MADE WITH VODKA

cranberry liqueur

PLAN AHEAD

This recipe needs
1 TO 3 WEEKS
steep time

This deep red liqueur makes for the most festive and beautiful wintertime cocktails! Cranberry liqueur only takes about 5 minutes to make, but does need one to three weeks of resting time to infuse the vodka.

INGREDIENTS

- 2 cups sugar
- 1 cup water
- 3 cups fresh or frozen cranberries (12 ounces)
- 3 cups vodka

DIRECTIONS

1. Combine the sugar and water in a saucepan and cook over medium heat, stirring regularly, until the sugar dissolves (about 5 minutes). Remove from the heat and allow it to cool to room temperature.
2. Using a food chopper, food processor, or knife, chop the cranberries until roughly chopped.
3. Combine the cooled sugar mixture, chopped cranberries, and vodka in a half-gallon jar with a well-fitting lid. Seal tightly and store in a cool, dark place for at least one full week, but preferably closer to 3 weeks, shaking every other day (or as often as you remember).
4. Strain the mixture through a cheesecloth-lined sieve, a nut milk bag, or a jelly bag. Pour the infused liquid into jars and store refrigerated or at room temperature for up to a year. Decorate the jars as desired (see page 11 for ideas) and tie on the tags.

MAKES 2 QUARTS LIMONCELLO

limoncello

PLAN AHEAD

This recipe needs
1 TO 6 WEEKS
steep time

If you've never had the pleasure of enjoying limoncello, you're in for a real treat! Limoncello is a traditional Italian liqueur made from lemons. The flavor is tart, citrusy, and sweet (thanks to the addition of simple syrup).

INGREDIENTS

- 10-14 organic lemons
- 750ml grain alcohol (like Everclear) or vodka
- 3 1/2 cups filtered water
- 3 cups granulated sugar

189/190-proof grain alcohol is preferable here, but if you only get 151- or 120-proof, that will also work. Vodka should be a last resort but will work in a pinch.

DIRECTIONS

1. Wash the lemons well, then peel into long strips—use a light touch, as you want to leave as much of the pith behind as possible. If using 190/189-proof grain alcohol, 10 lemons will be enough; for the other alcohols, you'll need to peel more lemons as the proof level decreases.
2. Using a sharp knife, scrape away the remaining white pith on the inside of the peels. Too much pith makes for a bitter end result.
3. Place the lemon peels in a half-gallon canning jar. Cover with the grain alcohol or vodka. Close lid and place in a spot out of direct sunlight. Shake daily. Infuse for at least one week (in the case of 190/189-proof alcohol) and up to six weeks (for the lower-proof alcohols). The infusion is ready when the alcohol is bright yellow and the lemon peels have lost most of their color.
4. When the infusion is ready, heat the water in a large saucepan over high heat. Whisk in the sugar and bring to a boil. Boil until the sugar is completely dissolved, about two minutes. Let simple syrup cool to room temperature.
5. Pour the simple syrup into the lemon infusion. Close the lid on the jar again, and shake well to combine. The mixture may turn cloudy (especially if using higher-proof alcohol)—this is completely fine.
6. Strain the lemon peels out of the limoncello through a fine-mesh sieve. Pour into jars. Decorate the jars as desired (see page 11 for ideas) and add the tags.

DOWNLOAD THE TAGS FOR THIS GIFT FOR FREE
zestmedia.co/giftsinjars

MAKE YOUR OWN

BLOODY MARY

Combine tomato juice, vodka, and seasoning packet over ice. Season with hot sauce to taste.

Cheers!

MAKES 1 QUART JAR EACH
enough for one large cocktail per jar

diy cocktail kits

I gave these cocktail kits to friends at a holiday party one year, and let me tell you, they were an absolute hit! The key to these kits is snagging the mini airplane bottles of liquor. I found the biggest selection of these at a big national alcohol retailer. If you can't source mini bottles of the liquor or the mixers, another option is to purchase small empty bottles online and fill them from a larger bottle of alcohol.

MOSCOW MULE

Place a bed of craft grass in the bottom of a wide-mouth quart jar. Fill jar with one mini can ginger beer, one mini vodka bottle, and either a small lime on top or a packet of crystallized lime.

OLD FASHIONED

Place a sugar cube inside a small zip-top bag. Place a bed of craft grass in the bottom of a wide-mouth quart jar. Fill a small dropper bottle with Angostura bitters and label. Fill jar with a mini bottle of bourbon, the sugar cube, the bitters, and a clementine.

COFFEE MARTINI

Place a bed of craft grass in the bottom of a wide-mouth quart jar. Fill jar with one mini bottle each of vodka (coffee or espresso flavored preferred), coffee liqueur, and Irish cream. Add one mini can of espresso or cold brew coffee.

MARGARITA

Place a bed of craft grass in the bottom of a wide-mouth quart jar. Fill jar with one mini can of margarita mix, one mini bottle of tequila, and one lime, for garnish. Affix lid, then tie ribbon or twine around the jar and attach the tag.

BLOODY MARY

Combine 1/2 teaspoon each celery salt, smoked paprika, and Worcestershire powder (available at online retailers) in a small zip-top bag. Place a bed of craft grass in the bottom of a wide-mouth quart jar. Fill jar with a mini can of tomato juice, one mini vodka bottle, a mini bottle of hot pepper sauce, and the seasoning packet.

TEQUILA SUNRISE

Fill a mini alcohol bottle with grenadine syrup. Place a bed of craft grass in the bottom of a wide-mouth quart jar. Fill jar with a mini bottle or juice box of orange juice, the grenadine syrup, and one mini bottle of tequila.

HANDMADE WITH ♡

Irish Cream

GREAT IN COFFEE!

irish cream

Homemade Irish cream is so much tastier than anything you can get from a bottle at the store! I love gifting Irish cream with a bag of local coffee and a nice mug to round out the gift.

PLAN AHEAD

This gift should stay refrigerated

INGREDIENTS

- 1 14-ounce can sweetened condensed milk
- 1 2/3 cups Irish whiskey, chilled
- 1 cup heavy cream
- 2 tablespoons chocolate syrup
- 1 1/2 teaspoon instant espresso granules
- 1 teaspoon vanilla extract
- 1/2 teaspoon almond extract

DIRECTIONS

1. Combine the ingredients in a blender and blend on low for 20-30 seconds until smooth. Alternatively, you can combine all ingredients in a large mixing bowl and whisk vigorously until smooth.
2. Pour into a quart-size canning jar. Keeps in the fridge for up to a month. Decorate the jar as desired (see page 11 for ideas) and tie on the tag.

protips

To prevent curdling, your whiskey must be chilled before adding it to the rest of the ingredients. Just pop it in the freezer an hour or two before you plan to make the recipe.

This Irish cream should stay refrigerated. You can take it out for an hour or two to gift it, but make sure your recipient knows it needs to head to the fridge afterward.

I've made a dairy-free version of this using sweetened condensed coconut milk (Nature's Charm brand) and dairy-free heavy whipping cream (Califia Farms brand). Make sure to select a chocolate syrup that does not contain milk. Nut milks (like almond or cashew) tend to curdle when mixed with the whiskey, so I cannot recommend those.

EVERYTHING BAGEL SEASONING • PAGE 96

for the cook

Have a foodie in your life? They'll love and appreciate the gift of these handmade ingredients for them to use during their culinary adventures. You might even inspire a new recipe!

GRILL SEASONINGS

EVERYTHING BAGEL SEASONING

RANCH SEASONING & DRESSING MIX

INFUSED FINISHING SALTS

VANILLA EXTRACT

SUN-DRIED TOMATOES

INFUSED OLIVE OIL

FLAVORED SUGARS

QUICK HOT SAUCE

PEELED GARLIC

grill seasonings

These two grill seasonings add tons of flavor to any item you'd put on the grill—one is packed with a citrus flavor that is perfect on fish and chicken, and the other has a rich, smoky profile that's great on pork and beef. Both are great options for veggies! Combine these spice rubs with a gift certificate for a meat subscription or some nice grill tools to round out the gift.

INGREDIENTS

for fish and chicken seasoning

- 3 tablespoons garlic powder
- 3 tablespoons onion powder
- 2 tablespoons lemon pepper
- 2 tablespoons sea salt
- 1 tablespoon dried parsley flakes
- 1 tablespoon ground coriander
- 2 teaspoons paprika
- 1 teaspoon turmeric
- 1/2 teaspoon red pepper flakes

for barbecue spice rub

- 1/3 cup sea salt
- 1/3 cup brown sugar or maple sugar
- 1/4 cup paprika
- 2 tablespoons black pepper
- 2 tablespoons dried oregano
- 1 tablespoon garlic powder
- 2 teaspoons dried thyme
- 1 teaspoon dried mustard
- 1/2 teaspoon cayenne pepper

DIRECTIONS

1. Whisk the ingredients together in a medium bowl until well combined.
2. Transfer to a half-pint canning jar. Decorate the jar as desired (see page 11 for ideas) and tie on the tag.

Handmade with ❤

**Everything
Bagel
Seasoning**

everything bagel seasoning

Imagine the savory flavor of an everything bagel, but on anything you want! This everything bagel seasoning is great on avocado toast, hard-boiled eggs, or even sprinkled onto roasted potatoes.

INGREDIENTS

- 1/4 cup poppy seeds
- 3 tablespoons dried minced garlic
- 3 tablespoons dried minced onion
- 2 tablespoons white sesame seeds
- 2 tablespoons black sesame seeds
- 4 teaspoons flaky sea salt

DIRECTIONS

1. Whisk together the ingredients in a medium bowl until well combined.
2. Transfer to a half-pint canning jar. Decorate the jar as desired (see page 11 for ideas) and tie on the tag.

Ranch Seasoning & Dressing Mix

To make ranch dressing: combine 3 tablespoons of this mix with 1 cup mayonnaise, 1/2 cup sour cream or plain Greek yogurt, 1/3 to 2/3 cup milk (depending on how thick you'd like your ranch), and juice of half a lemon (optional). Stir well, and refrigerate for at least 20 minutes before serving.

ranch seasoning & dressing mix

This homemade ranch mix is the perfect gift for the ranch lover in your life! Not only can you make a classic ranch dip or dressing with the mix, but you can also use the mix to add ranch flavor to anything you want.

INGREDIENTS

for the mix

- 1/2 cup buttermilk powder (available in the baking section of most supermarkets)
- 2 tablespoons dried parsley
- 1 tablespoon onion powder
- 1 tablespoon garlic powder
- 2 teaspoons dried chives
- 1 teaspoon dried dill
- 3/4 teaspoon fine sea salt
- 1/2 teaspoon pepper

for making dressing

- 3 tablespoons of mix
- 1 cup mayonnaise
- 1/2 cup sour cream or plain Greek yogurt
- 1/3 to 2/3 cup milk (depending on how thick you'd like your ranch)
- Juice of half a lemon (optional)

protip

Approximately three tablespoons of this mix equals one packet of store-bought ranch dressing mix.

DIRECTIONS

to make the mix

1. Whisk together the ingredients in a medium bowl until well combined.
2. Transfer to a half-pint canning jar. Decorate the jar as desired (see page 11 for ideas) and tie on the tag.

to make dressing

1. Combine all ingredients in a medium-sized bowl, using less milk if you'd like a thicker dip and more if you'd like a thinner dressing. Stir well, and refrigerate for at least 20 minutes before serving.

MAKES 1 PINT JAR EACH

infused finishing salts

These fancy salts not only look beautiful, but they also give an incredible burst of flavor to savory dishes. They are called "finishing salts" because you use them to finish a dish right before serving!

100

LEMON AND THYME

Preheat oven to 200°F. Combine 1 cup coarse or flaky salt, the zest from 2 lemons, and 2 tablespoons fresh thyme in a bowl until well combined. Spread the salt on a baking sheet lined with parchment paper and bake for one hour. Let cool completely, then transfer to a half-pint mason jar for storage.

SAGE AND ROSEMARY

Preheat oven to 200°F. Combine 1 cup coarse or flaky salt, 1/3 cup finely chopped fresh sage leaves, and 2 tablespoons finely chopped fresh rosemary leaves in a bowl until well combined. Spread the salt on a baking sheet lined with parchment paper and bake for one hour. Let cool completely, then transfer to a half-pint mason jar for storage.

CHIPOTLE AND LIME

Preheat oven to 200°F. Using a mortar and pestle, a spice grinder, or a small food processor, chop up 2 dried chipotle peppers until they are in small flakes. Stir with 1 cup coarse or flaky salt and the zest from 3 limes in a bowl until well combined. Spread the salt on a baking sheet lined with parchment paper and bake for one hour. Let cool completely, then transfer to a half-pint mason jar for storage.

HANDMADE *Vanilla Extr*

MAKES 1 HALF-PINT JAR

vanilla extract

PLAN AHEAD

**This recipe needs
6 TO 12
MONTHS
steep time**

Handmade vanilla extract is easy to make, but it does require up to a year of steeping time to be really delicious. I start a new batch each December so it's ready for gifting the following year.

INGREDIENTS

- 6 vanilla beans
- 8 ounces vodka, bourbon, brandy, or other high-proof alcohol

DIRECTIONS

1. Using a sharp knife, split the vanilla beans lengthwise from end to end. Place the split vanilla beans in a swing-top bottle or a small canning jar.
2. Pour the alcohol over the beans. Close the lid, and shake well. Place in a cool, dark spot to infuse for at least 8 weeks, but preferably up to 6-12 months. Shake daily (or as often as you remember).
3. The vanilla is ready to use when it is dark in color and strong in flavor.
4. Transfer to a half-pint canning jar. Decorate the jar as desired (see page 11 for ideas) and tie on the tag.

protip

Vodka is the standard choice for making vanilla, but other liquors are delicious as well. You can speed up the process by using high-proof grain alcohol, but know that the resulting extract has a stronger liquor flavor.

Sundried
Tomatoes

sun-dried tomatoes

I'm an avid vegetable gardener, and I love turning my garden bounty into thoughtful homemade gifts. These sun-dried tomatoes are one of my favorite garden gifts to give! They preserve the flavor of summer, but you can gift them anytime. Any cook would be thrilled to receive these!

INGREDIENTS

- Fresh tomatoes

DIRECTIONS

in the oven

1. Preheat your oven to 160°F. If your oven doesn't go that low, preheat it to as low as it will go, but know that you'll need to keep a close eye on your tomatoes to prevent burning.
2. Cut tomatoes into evenly sized pieces. For large tomatoes, quarter them. For medium, small, or cherry tomatoes, cut them into halves.
3. Place a baking rack inside a rimmed baking sheet. Place the tomatoes in a single layer on the baking rack.
4. Dry the tomatoes in the oven. It can help to flip your tomatoes over halfway through the drying process. If you have a few trays of tomatoes in your oven, crack the oven door to allow for better circulation. It will take several hours for the tomatoes to dry, and the exact time will depend on the size of your tomatoes, the humidity in the air, and other considerations. But a good rule of thumb is to start checking cherry tomatoes at the 2 hour mark and larger tomatoes at the 4-5 hour mark.
5. Your tomatoes are finished when they are dry but still pliable. Over-dried tomatoes will be brittle and tough. If tomatoes aren't dried long enough, they will spoil quickly. Make sure the tomatoes do not feel soft or moist.
6. Transfer to a quart canning jar. Decorate the jar as desired (see page 11 for ideas) and tie on the tag.

in a dehydrator

1. Cut tomatoes into evenly sized pieces. For large tomatoes, quarter them. For medium, small, or cherry tomatoes, cut them into halves.
2. Place the tomatoes in a single layer on dehydrator trays.
3. Dry the tomatoes in the dehydrator at 140°F. It will take several hours for the tomatoes to dry, and the exact time will depend on the size of your tomatoes, the humidity in the air, and other considerations. But a good rule of thumb is to start checking cherry tomatoes at the 2 hour mark and larger tomatoes at the 4-5 hour mark.
4. Your tomatoes are finished when they are dry but still pliable. Over-dried tomatoes will be brittle and tough. If tomatoes aren't dried long enough, they will spoil quickly. Make sure the tomatoes do not feel soft or moist.
5. Transfer to a quart canning jar. Decorate the jar as desired (see page 11 for ideas) and tie on the tag.

BASIL & SUNDRIED TOMATO
Extra Virgin Olive Oil

infused olive oil

PLAN AHEAD

This gift needs to stay refrigerated

These infused olive oils are beautiful and useful! They make a wonderful base to a salad dressing and they add so much flavor to a simple pasta dish.

INGREDIENTS

rosemary and garlic olive oil

- About 2 cups extra virgin olive oil
- 2 sprigs fresh rosemary
- 4 cloves peeled garlic
- 1 tablespoon whole peppercorns

basil and sun-dried tomato olive oil

- About 2 cups extra virgin olive oil
- 1/3 cup sun-dried tomatoes (see page 104)
- 1 loosely packed cup fresh basil leaves
- 2 cloves peeled garlic

chile lime olive oil

- About 2 cups extra virgin olive oil
- 3 dried small chile peppers (1 teaspoon of red pepper flakes also works)
- Peel of 1 lime
- 1 tablespoon whole peppercorns

DIRECTIONS

1. Place the non-oil ingredients in the bottom of a pint jar. Set the jar onto a wooden cutting board or clean kitchen towel.
2. Warm the olive oil in a saucepan over low heat until it begins to bubble gently.
3. Remove from heat, and pour the warm oil over the ingredients in the jar until it reaches the top of the jar. Cover the jar and shake well.
4. Leave out at room temperature for 1-2 hours, then move the jars to the fridge for at least a week.
5. Decorate the jar as desired (see page 11 for ideas) and tie on the tag. Bring to room temperature for 20-30 minutes before enjoying.

protip

Because these recipes use fresh ingredients for infusion, it's important to store the finished olive oil in the refrigerator. Just put it out on the counter for 20-30 minutes before you'd like to use it to bring it back to liquid form. You can leave it out of the fridge for up to 8 hours for the purpose of gift-giving—just make sure your recipient knows to store it in the fridge afterward. Infused oils can be safely used for up to a year if refrigerated.

PLAN AHEAD

These need
1 WEEK
infusion time

HANDMADE
Flavored Sugar
VANILLA

HANDMADE
Flavored Sugar
GINGER

HANDMADE
Flavored Sugar
LAVENDER

MAKES 1 PINT JAR EACH

GF DF V VG

flavored sugars

These infused sugars add a hint of flavor to coffee or tea. They are great sprinkled onto baked goods right before they go in the oven. These are a thoughtful gift for any baker in your life.

ESPRESSO

Combine 1 1/2 cups granulated sugar and 1/2 cup espresso roast whole coffee beans in a medium-sized bowl. Transfer the sugar into a pint-size canning jar. Close and set in a cool, dark place (not the fridge) for at least a week before enjoying.

VANILLA

Cut 2 vanilla beans in half lengthwise. Open each half up and using the back of a spoon, scrape out the vanilla bean seeds into a a bowl with 2 cups of sugar. Rub the vanilla bean seeds into the sugar to break apart the clumps and combine. Transfer the sugar into a pint-size canning jar, adding the scraped whole vanilla beans as you fill. Close and set in a cool, dark place (not the fridge) for at least a week before enjoying.

CINNAMON

Combine 1 1/2 cups granulated sugar and 1/2 cup ground cinnamon in a medium-sized bowl. Transfer the sugar into a pint-size canning jar. Close and set in a cool, dark place (not the fridge) for at least a week before enjoying.

GINGER

Combine 2 cups granulated sugar and 1/3 cup chopped crystallized ginger in a medium-sized bowl. Transfer the sugar into a pint-size canning jar. Close and set in a cool, dark place (not the fridge) for at least a week before enjoying.

LAVENDER

Combine 2 cups granulated sugar and 1/4 cup dried lavender buds in a medium-sized bowl. Transfer the sugar into a pint-size canning jar. Close and set in a cool, dark place (not the fridge) for at least a week before enjoying.

CITRUS

Combine 2 cups sugar with 1/4 cup fresh orange, lime, or lemon zest in a medium-sized bowl Rub the zest into the sugar to break apart the clumps and combine. Transfer the sugar into a pint-size canning jar. Close and set in a cool, dark place (not the fridge) for at least a week before enjoying. **109**

MAKES 4 PINTS

quick hot sauce

PLAN AHEAD

This gift needs to stay refrigerated

Traditional hot sauce is made through fermentation, but if you're looking for a quicker alternative, this cooked hot sauce is the one for you! It does need to stay refrigerated, but you can bring it out of the fridge for a few hours for gift-giving purposes.

INGREDIENTS

- 1 1/2 pounds peppers of your choosing (a mix of sweet peppers and hot peppers), tops/stems removed, halved
- 6 cloves garlic, peeled
- 4 cups filtered water, divided
- 4 teaspoons sea salt, divided
- 1/3 cup apple cider vinegar
- 1 tablespoon honey or maple syrup, optional
- 1/2 teaspoon xanthan gum, optional (see notes)

DIRECTIONS

1. Combine the peppers, garlic, 2 cups of water, 2 teaspoons of sea salt, apple cider vinegar, and honey or maple syrup (if using) in a medium pan over medium-high heat. Bring to a boil, reduce heat, and simmer for 10-15 minutes, or until the peppers and garlic have softened.
2. Pour mixture into a blender. Make sure to leave the cover vent open, but covered with a kitchen towel, and blend until very smooth.
3. While the blender is running, sprinkle in the xanthan gum, if using, and blend for an additional minute.
4. Transfer mixture to pint jars. Decorate the jars as desired (see page 11 for ideas) and apply the tags. Store in the fridge for up to a month.

protips

You can use a mix of whatever peppers you like to achieve your perfect spice level and flavor. My only recommendation is to stick to the same color family—mixing green and red peppers will leave you with an unpleasant brown-colored hot sauce.

In this recipe, xanthan gum works as an emulsifier, stabilizer, and thickener. It is 100% optional. If you choose not to use it, your hot sauce will separate in the fridge. Just give it a good shake each time you go to use it.

READY-TO-USE
Peeled Garlic

MAKES 1 QUART

peeled garlic

PLAN AHEAD

This gift needs to stay refrigerated

I consider this one of the most thoughtful gifts in the entire book because if you are a cook, you know just how much time a whole jar of peeled garlic will save you! I like to do this after I harvest my garlic crop from the garden each year. I store dozens of jars of garlic in the back of my fridge to use and to gift all year long.

INGREDIENTS

- 6-10 heads of garlic, depending on size
- 2-4 cups white wine vinegar

DIRECTIONS

1. Peel the garlic. This is a labor of love that any cook will appreciate, but to make it a little easier, break apart your cloves and put them in a large metal bowl. Cover the bowl with a pot lid or a second similarly sized bowl, and shake vigorously for 20-30 seconds, until most of the peels come off.
2. Fill a quart jar with the peeled garlic cloves. Cover with the white wine vinegar. Put on the lid and store in the refrigerator for up to a year.

protip

The white wine vinegar left in the jar makes a wonderful garlic-infused vinegar for salad dressings!

GLUTEN-FREE PIZZA CRUST MIX • PAGE 132

dinners

Give the gift of a quick and easy dinner with these meals-in-a-jar! Each jar takes just a few minutes to put together. To fill out the gift, I love pairing these jars with some cute kitchen utensils or towels.

COCONUT CURRY SOUP MIX

BLACK BEAN SOUP MIX

SPLIT PEA SOUP MIX

CHICKEN NOODLE SOUP MIX

THREE-BEAN CHILI MIX

FIVE-BEAN SOUP MIX

ITALIAN BARLEY SOUP MIX

GARLIC & HERB PIZZA CRUST MIX

GLUTEN-FREE PIZZA CRUST MIX

coconut curry soup mix

This lentil soup is bright orange, packed full of rich flavor, and super delicious served with a stack of warm naan bread! This soup is also vegan and gluten-free.

INGREDIENTS

for the mix

- 2/3 cup orange lentils
- 2/3 cup green lentils
- 1 tablespoon curry powder
- 1 tablespoon dried chopped onions
- 1 tablespoon dried minced garlic
- 2 veggie bouillon cubes
- 1 small dried chile pepper

protip

This mix can be doubled to fit into a quart-sized jar and make 8 servings.

for the soup

- Jar of soup mix
- 1 15-ounce can full-fat coconut milk
- 4 cups water

DIRECTIONS

to make the mix jars

1. Layer all ingredients in the order listed in a pint-size wide-mouth mason jar.
2. Decorate the jar as desired (see page 11 for ideas) and tie on the tag.

to make the soup

1. Remove wrapper from bouillon cube and add it, plus all remaining ingredients in the jar, to a saucepan. Add four cups of water and the can of coconut milk.
2. Bring to a boil over high heat, reduce heat to low, and simmer until the lentils are tender, about 20 minutes. Remove and discard the chile pepper before serving. Season to taste.

black bean soup mix

This soup is the ultimate comfort food! I like serving it topped with sour cream, chopped avocado, and fresh minced cilantro. Cornbread is also amazing on the side!

INGREDIENTS

for the mix

- 4 chicken or veggie bouillon cubes, unwrapped
- 2 bay leaves
- 2 tablespoons ground cumin
- 1 tablespoon dried onion flakes
- 1 tablespoon chili powder
- 2 teaspoons garlic powder
- 1 teaspoon celery seed
- 1/2 teaspoon crushed red pepper flakes
- 1/2 teaspoon black pepper
- 3 1/2 cups dried black beans (about 1 1/2 pounds)

for the soup

- Jar of soup mix
- Water

DIRECTIONS

to make the mix jars

1. Lay out a 12" x 12" piece of parchment paper. Place the bouillon cubes, bay leaves, cumin, onion flakes, chili powder, garlic powder, celery seed, red pepper flakes, and black pepper in the center of the paper. Roll up the sides to make a packet, and secure the packet closed with a rubber band.
2. Fill a wide-mouth quart jar with the dried black beans. Stuff the closed packet into the top of the jar. Close the jar and decorate as desired (see page 11 for ideas). Tie on the tag.

protip

This gift jar requires you to make a spice packet out of parchment paper. No worries, it's easy! Just fold up the spices and secure the packet with a rubber band. You can also use a small zip-top bag if that's easier.

to make the soup

1. Pull out the spice packet and set aside. Pour the black beans into a large bowl and cover with water. Let soak for at least six hours or overnight.
2. After soaking time, drain the beans and then add them to a large stock pot or Dutch oven along with the contents of the spice packet and 12 cups of water.
3. Bring to a boil over high heat. Reduce heat and simmer for 1 1/2 to 2 hours, stirring occasionally, until the beans are tender and the soup is thick. Remove the bay leaves before serving.

split pea soup mix

This beautiful green soup mix is so simple yet delicious! I like to stir in a cup of chopped ham when it's finished cooking to make it really hearty.

INGREDIENTS

for the mix
- 2 cups split green peas
- 1/2 teaspoon celery seed
- 1 tablespoon dried chopped onions
- 1 tablespoon dried minced garlic
- 1 bay leaf
- 1 chicken bouillon cube

protip

This mix can be doubled to fit into a quart-sized jar and make 8 servings.

for the soup
- Jar of soup mix
- 4 cups water
- 1 cup chopped ham

DIRECTIONS

to make the mix jars
1. Layer all ingredients in the order listed in a pint-size wide-mouth mason jar.
2. Decorate the jar as desired (see page 11 for ideas) and tie on the tag.

to make the soup
1. Remove wrapper from bouillon cube and add it, plus all remaining ingredients in the jar, to a saucepan. Add four cups of water.
2. Bring to a boil over high heat, reduce heat to low, and simmer until the peas are tender, about 30 minutes.
3. Remove and discard the bay leaf. Stir in one cup of chopped ham before serving. Season to taste.

chicken noodle soup mix

This chicken noodle soup starter jar is the perfect gift to give to someone who is feeling under the weather.

INGREDIENTS

for the mix

- 1 tablespoon dried chopped onions
- 1 tablespoon dried minced garlic
- 1 bay leaf
- 1/2 teaspoon dried rosemary
- 1/2 teaspoon dried sage
- 1/2 teaspoon dried thyme
- 1/2 teaspoon celery seed
- 1 chicken bouillon cube
- 2 cups wide egg noodles

for the soup

- 1 tablespoon olive oil
- 1 large carrot, peeled and diced
- 1 large stalk celery, diced
- Jar of soup mix
- 3 cups water
- 2 cup diced, cooked chicken

protip

This mix can be doubled to fit into a quart-sized jar and make 8 servings.

DIRECTIONS

to make the mix jars

1. Layer all ingredients in the order listed in a pint-size wide-mouth mason jar.
2. Decorate the jar as desired (see page 11 for ideas) and tie on the tag.

to make the soup

1. Heat 1 tablespoon oil in a saucepan over medium-high heat. Sauté one diced carrot and one diced celery stalk until just tender, about 5 minutes.
2. Unwrap the bouillon cube from the soup mix, and then add it, plus all remaining ingredients in the jar, to the saucepan. Add 3 cups of water. Bring to a boil, reduce heat, and simmer until the noodles are cooked through, about 10 minutes.
3. Remove bay leaf. Stir in 2 cups chopped cooked chicken before serving. Season to taste.

HANDMADE WITH

3-Bean Chili Mix

Slow Cooker Directions: Brown 1 pound of ground beef, drain fat, and then combine the beef with the chili mix, 12 cups of water, 1 can of diced tomatoes, and 1 can of tomato paste in a slow cooker and cook on high for 8 hours until beans are tender.

Instant Pot Directions: Brown 1 pound of ground beef, drain fat, and then combine the beef with the chili mix, 12 cups of water, 1 can diced tomatoes, and 1 can tomato paste in the Instant Pot. Seal and cool on Manual/High for 30 minutes with a natural press release.

MUIR GLEN
ORGANIC
TOMATO
NET WT 6

MU
OF

PETITE D
TOMATOE
NET WT 14.5 OZ (411g)

each jar makes 8 servings chili

three-bean chili mix

Give the gift of a warm, cozy, comforting meal with this chili mix! Gift the jar solo, or package it into a basket with the canned tomatoes needed for the recipe, plus some cute bowls and spoons.

INGREDIENTS

for the jar

- 2/3 cup dried black beans
- 2/3 cup dried pinto beans
- 2/3 cup dried white beans (not cannellini beans)
- 2 tablespoons dried minced onion
- 1 packet (1/4 cup) dried veggie soup mix (like Knorr)
- 2 tablespoons chili powder
- 2 tablespoons ground cumin
- 1 tablespoon paprika
- 1 teaspoon sea salt
- 1/2 teaspoon black pepper
- 2 beef bouillon cubes, unwrapped

for the chili

- 1 pound ground beef
- 8 cups water (2 empty mix jars' worth)
- 1 15-ounce can diced tomatoes
- 1 6-ounce can tomato paste

protips

Do not replace any of the beans in this chili mix with kidney beans or cannellini (white kidney) beans. Dry kidney and cannellini beans contain high levels of a compound that causes some folks to have digestive issues, and most slow cookers do not get hot enough to kill the toxin.

A one-pound bag of each type of beans will be enough for three batches of chili mix.

Heads up: most vegetable soup mixes contain traces of milk and gluten. so this gift isn't suitable for recipients who avoid gluten and dairy.

DIRECTIONS

to make the mix jars

1. Layer all ingredients in the order listed in a quart-size wide-mouth mason jar.
2. Decorate the jar as desired (see page 11 for ideas) and tie on the tag.

to make the chili

1. **Slow Cooker:** Brown ground beef (either in the slow cooker on a sauté setting or on the stove) and drain the fat. Combine the beef with the chili mix, water, diced tomatoes, and tomato paste in a slow cooker and cook on High for 8 hours, until the beans are tender.
2. **Instant Pot:** Brown ground beef on sauté setting in Instant Pot and drain the fat. Combine the beef with the chili mix, water, diced tomatoes, and tomato paste in the Instant Pot. Seal and cook on Manual/High for 30 minutes with a natural pressure release.

five-bean soup mix

I think this is one of the most beautiful jars in the entire book! Layers of brightly-colored beans look so enticing. This is a vegetarian soup, but it's still packed with awesome flavor.

INGREDIENTS

for the mix

- 1/3 cup dried pinto beans
- 1/3 cup green peas
- 1/3 cup dried black beans
- 1/3 cup dried great Northern beans
- 1/3 cup dried kidney beans
- 1 teaspoon dry mustard
- 1 teaspoon paprika
- 1 tablespoon dried chopped onions
- 1 tablespoon dried garlic powder
- 1 tablespoon dried oregano
- 1 bay leaf
- 1 small dried chile pepper (optional)
- 1 teaspoon dried rosemary
- 1 veggie bouillon cubes

for the soup

- Jar of soup mix
- 5 cups water
- 1 14-ounce can diced tomatoes

protip

This mix can be doubled to fit into a quart-sized jar and make 8 servings.

You might be tempted to make this soup in the slow cooker, but dry kidney and cannellini beans contain high levels of a compound that causes some folks to have digestive issues, and most slow cookers do not get hot enough to kill the toxin.

DIRECTIONS

to make the mix jars

1. Layer all ingredients in the order listed in a pint-size wide-mouth mason jar.
2. Decorate the jar as desired (see page 11 for ideas) and tie on the tag.

to make the soup

1. Remove wrapper from bouillon cube and add it, plus all remaining ingredients from the jar, five cups of water, and one 14-ounce can of diced tomatoes to a saucepan.
2. Bring to a boil over high heat, reduce heat to low, and simmer until the beans are tender and the soup is thick, about 90 minutes, adding more water as necessary to soften the beans.
3. Remove and discard chile pepper and bay leaf before serving. Season to taste.

italian barley soup mix

This barley soup is tomato-based (you add a can of diced tomatoes when cooking), vegetarian, and packed with garlic and Italian herbs! Serve it with some garlic bread and a nice side salad to round out the meal.

INGREDIENTS

for the mix

- 1 cup pearled barley
- 1/2 cup sun-dried tomatoes (see page 104)
- 1 tablespoon dried chopped onions
- 1 tablespoon dried minced garlic
- 2 tablespoons dried basil
- 1 tablespoon dried oregano
- 1 tablespoon dried parsley flakes
- 1 veggie bouillon cube

for the soup

- Jar of soup mix
- 5 cups water
- 1 14-ounce can diced tomatoes

protips

This mix can be doubled to fit into a quart-sized jar and make 8 servings.

To keep this jar shelf-stable, be sure to use dehydrated sun-dried tomatoes, *not* sun-dried tomatoes packed in oil.

DIRECTIONS

to make the mix jars

1. Layer all ingredients in the order listed in a pint-size wide-mouth mason jar.
2. Decorate the jar as desired (see page 11 for ideas) and tie on the tag.

to make the soup

1. Remove wrapper from bouillon cube and add it, plus all remaining ingredients from the jar, five cups of water, and one 14-ounce can of diced tomatoes to a saucepan.
2. Bring to a boil over high heat, reduce heat to low, and simmer until the barley is tender and the soup is thick, about 20 minutes. Season to taste.

GARLIC + HERB
Pizza Crust
makes 1– 12" crust

YOU'LL NEED:
2 cups mix
2 tablespoons olive oil
(plus more for drizzling)
3/4 cup warm water
(around 110°F)

TO MAKE:
1. Add mix, oil and water into a large bowl and stir well very well. The dough will still be sticky.
2. Drizzle a separate, large bowl generously with olive oil. Transfer your dough ball to the new bowl, and then rotate the dough to coat in oil. Cover the bowl with plastic wrap and place it in a warm place to rise until doubled in size—about 30-60 minutes.
3. Preheat oven to 425 degrees. Line a pizza pan or baking sheet with parchment paper.
4. Dump out the dough onto a floured surface and form into a 12" circle. Transfer the dough to the parchment-lined baking sheet.
5. Add desired toppings and bake in preheated oven for 13-15 minutes or until toppings are golden brown.

garlic & herb pizza crust mix

This pizza crust mix makes for such easy pizza nights! Just mix it with olive oil and water, let it rise, and you'll have homemade pizza in no time.

INGREDIENTS

for the mix

- 6 cups all-purpose flour
- 2 tablespoons instant yeast
- 2 tablespoons salt
- 1 tablespoon granulated sugar
- 1 teaspoon garlic powder
- 1 teaspoon Italian seasoning

for the crust

- 2 cups mix
- 2 tablespoons olive oil, plus more for drizzling
- 3/4 cup warm—not hot—water (around 110°F)

DIRECTIONS

to make the mix jars

1. Mix all ingredients in a large bowl, whisking to combine thoroughly.
2. Transfer mix to a half-gallon mason jar and close lid.
3. Decorate the jar as desired (see page 11 for ideas) and tie on the tag.

to make the crust

1. Add mix, oil, and water to a large bowl and stir very well. The dough will still be sticky. Form into a ball the best you can.
2. Drizzle a separate, large bowl generously with olive oil. Transfer your dough ball to the new bowl, and then rotate the dough to coat in oil. Cover the bowl with plastic wrap and place it in a warm place to rise until doubled in size—about 30-60 minutes.
3. Preheat oven to 425°F. Line a pizza pan or baking sheet with parchment paper.
4. Dump the dough out onto a floured surface and form into a 12" circle. Transfer the dough to the parchment-lined baking sheet.
5. Add desired toppings and bake in preheated oven for 13-15 minutes, or until toppings are golden brown.

Gluten Free Pizza Crust

makes 1–14" crust

YOU'LL NEED:
2 1/2 cups mix
1 1/2 cups warm water
(around 110°F)
1/2 cup olive oil

TO MAKE:
1. Add the mix and water to a bowl, and stir until well combined. Let dough rest for a couple minutes, then add in the olive oil and mix until well combined. The dough will be thick and sticky.
2. Cover bowl with plastic wrap and place in a warm area to rise until just puffy—about 30-60 minutes.
3. After rising time is up, preheat oven to 425°F degrees. Using oiled hands, spread the dough into a parchment-covered baking sheet or pizza pan.
4. Bake the crust for 13-15 minutes or until it's evenly browned all over.
5. Top with pizza sauce, toppings, and cheese. Bake for another 10-12 minutes or until cheese is melty and browned.

gluten-free pizza crust mix

This is hands-down the best gluten-free pizza crust I've ever had! It's fluffy on the inside and crispy on the outside. Because this crust mix is gluten-free, dairy-free, and vegan, this is a wonderful gift for those people in your life who eat a specialty diet.

INGREDIENTS

for the mix

- 7 1/2 cups gluten-free flour blend with xanthan gum
- 4 teaspoons instant yeast
- 3 tablespoons gluten-free baking powder
- 3 tablespoons granulated sugar
- 3 teaspoons salt

for the crust

- 2 1/2 cups mix
- 1 1/2 cups warm—not hot—water (around 110°F)
- 1/2 cup olive oil

protip

Gluten-free flours vary widely, but I've found this recipe to be pretty flexible when it comes to different flour brands. I tested this recipe with Better Batter All-Purpose Gluten-Free Blend with great results.

DIRECTIONS

to make the mix jars

1. Mix all ingredients in a large bowl, whisking to combine thoroughly.
2. Transfer mix to a half-gallon mason jar and close lid.
3. Decorate the jar as desired (see page 11 for ideas) and tie on the tag.

to make the crust

1. Add the mix and water to a bowl, and stir until well combined. You can do this by hand, but I've had the best luck making this in a stand mixer or with a hand mixer. Let dough rest for a couple of minutes, then add in the olive oil and mix until well combined. The dough will be thick and sticky.
2. Cover bowl with plastic wrap and place in a warm area to rise until just puffy—about 30-60 minutes.
3. After rising time is up, preheat oven to 425°F. Using oiled hands, spread the dough onto a parchment-covered baking sheet or pizza pan.
4. Bake the crust for 13-15 minutes, or until it's evenly browned all over.
5. Top with pizza sauce, toppings, and cheese. Bake for another 10-12 minutes, or until cheese is melty and browned.

RED ONION JAM • PAGE 148

canned goods

Yes, you can can! Water bath canning is surprisingly straightforward, and you don't need any special tools to do it safely. I'll show you how in this chapter, plus give you a few of my favorite fancy (but easy!) canning recipes that are perfect for gift-giving.

BERRY SYRUPS

BOURBON PEACH JAM

POMEGRANATE JELLY

SPICED APPLE BUTTER

RED ONION JAM

MUSTARD FLIGHT

PICKLED BEETS

canning 101

Even for those of us who are well-versed in the kitchen, water bath canning can be intimidating. But I promise, once you know the basics, canning is safe, easy, and fun!

HOW DOES THE CANNING PROCESS WORK?

water bath canning works by processing foods at a high temperature to destroy any microorganisms that could spoil the food. This heating process and the associated cooling process seal the lids of the jars with a tight suction similar to what you see in store-purchased shelf-stable foods. This vacuum seal prevents air from entering the canned goods, which could bring along new microorganisms that cause spoilage. The resulting canned goods are now shelf-stable!

protip

There is another type of canning —pressure canning—designed for canning low-acid foods, but we won't be using that process for any recipes in this book.

WHAT TOOLS DO YOU NEED TO CAN?

Canning does require a few specialty tools to make the process safer and easier. Here's what you need:

- Canning rack or trivet
- Jar lifter
- Headspace tool or plastic ruler
- Canning funnel
- Ladle
- Jars
- Lid rings
- Flat lids (these must be new for each canning batch)
- A large canning pot or stock pot

protip

You must follow the jar size listed in the canning recipe to ensure your food is shelf-stable.

HOW LONG DO HOMEMADE CANNED GOODS LAST?

Properly sealed canned goods are best used within 18 months. However, as long as the jar still has a good seal, canned goods can be stored almost indefinitely. The quality of the food might decrease (you might lose flavor, color, or texture), but it will still be safe to eat.

protip

I try to can one or two batches of something special each year to have stocked in my pantry for last-minute host or hostess gifts.

ADJUSTING FOR ALTITUDE

Live at a higher altitude? You'll need to process your canned goods for longer to ensure they are shelf-stable. Here's how much time to add to your processing time.

1,001 ft – 3,000 ft	Add **5 MINUTES** to processing time
3,001 ft – 6,000 ft	Add **10 MINUTES** to processing time
6,001 ft – 8,000 ft	Add **15 MINUTES** to processing time
8,001 ft+	Add **20 MINUTES** to processing time

1 Wash Jars and Lids

Wash all the jars, lids, and rings in warm, soapy water. The jars themselves can go in the dishwasher, but the lids and rings must be cleaned by hand. The rings and jars can be reused from previous canning batches, but the flat lids must be new for each recipe.

2 Prep the Canner

Fill your canning pot with enough water to cover the jars by at least an inch. Fit the canning rack or trivet into the bottom and then lower the jars into the water. While you prepare your canning recipe, bring the canner to just a simmer to keep the jars warm—don't let it come to a full boil just yet.

3 Prepare the Recipe

While the canner warms up, start prepping whatever you are canning. It's important to follow the recipe exactly so you can be sure the final result is safe to can. Do not change amounts or tweak the recipe in any way.

4 Fill the Jars

Working one jar at a time and using your jar lifter, bring a jar out of the water, and drain the water back into the canning pot. Place the jar on a kitchen towel or wooden cutting board, and fit it with a canning funnel. Ladle your recipe into the jar.

5 Check and Adjust Headspace

Remove the funnel to check the headspace—the amount of empty space between the top of the food and the top rim of the jar. The amount of headspace will be listed in the recipe. Run a rubber spatula along the inside of the jar to release any air bubbles, then check the headspace with your headspace checker or a clean plastic ruler, and adjust the level as needed.

6 Wipe Rims

Wipe down the rim of your jar with a damp cloth or paper towel. If there is any food left where the lid meets the jar, it could interfere with getting a good seal.

7 Attach Lids and Rings

Center a flat lid on top of the jar, and then screw on the ring. Tighten to just fingertip tight. Over-tightening your lids can make it so they cannot seal properly, and the lids may buckle and warp during processing. Return the jar to the canner.

8 Process

Once all your jars are filled and back in the canner, put the lid back on the canning pot, and bring the water to a boil. Your recipe will tell you what the processing time needs to be—don't start that timer until the water is at a full boil.

9 Rest and Remove from Canner

When the time is up, turn off the heat and remove the lid from the canning pot. Leave the jars there for five minutes, and then use your jar lifter to move them to a thick towel or wooden cutting board to cool. Be sure to leave an inch or two between the jars so that they cool evenly.

10 Cool, Check Seals, and Store

After the jars have cooled, confirm that all the jars have been sealed by pressing a finger into the middle of each lid. If the lid flexes, the jar didn't seal and should go directly into the fridge. If the lid doesn't flex, the jar is sealed and shelf-stable. Remove the rings, wipe down the jars, and label your preserves. They are ready for long-term storage!

Blueberry
Syrup

GREAT ON PANCAKES
AND ICE CREAM!

HANDMADE WITH

Strawberry
Syrup

GREAT ON PANCAKE
AND ICE CREAM!

berry syrups

These syrups are great drizzled on pancakes, waffles, or ice cream! I love adding a couple tablespoons to some seltzer water for a delicious mocktail. For gifting, pair a jar of berry syrup with a jar of Whole Grain Pancake Mix (page 34) for a wonderful breakfast basket.

INGREDIENTS

- 6 1/2 cups fresh or frozen blueberries, raspberries, or strawberries (or a combination)
- 4 1/2 cups granulated sugar
- 3/4 cup additional fresh or frozen berries, chopped, optional (if you'd like whole fruit chunks in your syrup)

DIRECTIONS

1. Prepare water bath canner, jars, and lids per steps on page 138.
2. Wash and remove stems/caps from fruit and crush in a large saucepan. Heat to boiling over medium-high heat, and simmer until very soft (about 5-10 minutes).
3. Remove from heat, and strain the fruit mixture through a fine-mesh sieve into a large glass measuring cup. When it is cool enough to handle, strain the remaining pulp in the sieve through a double layer of cheesecloth, a jelly bag, or a nut milk bag. Measure out 3 cups of juice. Discard the dry pulp.
4. Combine the 3 cups of juice with the sugar in a large saucepan. If you'd like your syrup to have chunks of whole fruit, add the additional 3/4 cup of fruit at this point. Bring to a boil and simmer for 1 minute, until all sugar is dissolved.
5. Remove syrup from heat. Ladle hot syrup into a hot jar, leaving a 1/2-inch headspace. Remove air bubbles and confirm proper headspace. Wipe the jar rim clean and center a flat lid on the jar. Apply the band and adjust to fingertip-tight. Place the jar in the boiling water canner. Repeat until all jars are filled.
6. Process jars for 10 minutes, adjusting for altitude (page 136). Turn off the heat, remove the canner lid, and let the jars stand for 5 minutes. Move the jars to a thick towel or wooden cutting board on the counter, and let them cool for 12-24 hours. Do not retighten any rings that have loosened.
7. Once cool, press on the center of each lid to make sure the jar is sealed properly—the lid should not flex at all when pressed.
8. Wipe down the jars and decorate as desired (see page 11 for ideas). Tie on the tags.

DOWNLOAD THE TAGS FOR THIS GIFT FOR FREE
zestmedia.co/giftsinjars

bourbon peach jam

Fancy jams are one of my favorite gifts to give! They can help elevate a grilled cheese or charcuterie board, and they have unique flavor combinations that you can't find in the store. It doesn't hurt that they are a breeze to make! This Bourbon Peach Jam is ready in less than an hour.

INGREDIENTS

- 4 pounds fresh peaches, peeled
- 6 tablespoons powdered pectin
- 1/4 cup bottled lemon juice
- 1/4 cup bourbon
- 2 tablespoons finely chopped crystallized ginger
- 7 cups sugar

protip

Do not use this recipe to can white-flesh peaches. Some varieties of white-flesh peaches are lower in acid, making them unsafe for water bath canning. Stick with yellow peaches for this recipe.

DIRECTIONS

1. Prepare water bath canner, jars, and lids per steps on page 138.
2. Pit and coarsely chop peaches. Measure out 4 1/2 cups chopped peaches and pour into a large saucepan or enameled Dutch oven. Mash with a potato masher until evenly crushed. Stir in pectin, lemon juice, bourbon, and crystallized ginger.
3. Heat pan over high heat, and stirring constantly, bring mixture to a rolling boil that cannot be stirred down.
4. Once at a full rolling boil, add the sugar, stirring to dissolve. Return mixture to a full rolling boil. Boil hard for 1 minute, stirring constantly. Remove from heat and skim off any foam if necessary.
5. Ladle hot jam into a hot jar, leaving 1/4-inch headspace. Remove air bubbles and confirm proper headspace. Wipe the jar rim clean and center a flat lid on the jar. Apply the band and adjust to fingertip-tight. Place the jar in the boiling water canner. Repeat until all jars are filled.
6. Process jars for 10 minutes, adjusting time for altitude (see page 136). Turn off the heat, remove the canner lid, and let the jars stand for 5 minutes. Move the jars to a thick towel or wooden cutting board on the counter, and let them cool for 12-24 hours. Do not retighten any rings that have loosened.
7. Once cool, press on the center of each lid to make sure the jar sealed properly—the lid should not flex at all when pressed.
8. Wipe down the jars and decorate as desired (see page 11 for ideas). Tie on the tags.

pomegranate jelly

This Pomegranate Jelly couldn't be easier to make! The secret ingredient is store-bought pomegranate juice, which takes all the tedious work out of preparing this recipe.

INGREDIENTS

- 3 1/2 cups bottled pomegranate juice
- 6 tablespoons powdered pectin
- 1/2 teaspoon butter, optional
- 5 cups sugar

DIRECTIONS

1. Prepare water bath canner, jars, and lids per steps on page 138.
2. Pour pomegranate juice into a large saucepan or stockpot. Gradually stir in the pectin until well combined.
3. Add 1/2 teaspoon of butter to the juice to reduce foaming while cooking, if desired. Heat pan over high heat, and, stirring constantly, bring the juice mixture to a rolling boil that cannot be stirred down.
4. Once the juice is at a full rolling boil, add the sugar, stirring to dissolve. Return the juice to a full rolling boil. Boil hard for 1 minute, stirring constantly, and then remove from the heat. Skim off any foam if necessary.
5. Ladle hot jelly into hot jars, leaving 1/4-inch headspace. Remove air bubbles and confirm proper headspace. Wipe the jar rim clean and center a flat lid on the jar. Apply the band and adjust to fingertip-tight. Place the jar in the boiling water canner. Repeat until all jars are filled.
6. Boil jars for 10 minutes, adjusting time for altitude (see page 136). Turn off the heat, remove the canner lid, and let the jars stand for 5 minutes. Move the jars to a thick towel or wooden cutting board on the counter, and let them cool for 12-24 hours. Do not retighten any rings that have loosened.
7. Once cool, press on the center of each lid to make sure the jar is sealed properly—the lid should not flex at all when pressed.
8. Wipe down the jars and decorate as desired (see page 11 for ideas). Tie on the tags.

spiced apple butter

Indulge in the warm flavors of autumn with this delightful spiced apple butter recipe. Perfect for spreading on toast or adding to a bowl of oatmeal, this is a wonderful gift for anyone on your list.

INGREDIENTS

- 4 pounds apples (about 12 to 16 medium apples)
- 2 cups water
- 3 cups granulated sugar
- 1 cup brown sugar
- 1/4 cup bottled lemon juice
- 2 teaspoons ground cinnamon
- 1/2 teaspoon ground ginger
- 1/4 teaspoon ground cloves
- 1/4 teaspoon ground nutmeg

protips

Use whatever apples you like and have on hand. I typically use about half tart apples (like Granny Smith) and half sweet apples (like Gala).

No need to peel the apples! The cooking process breaks the peels down, so save yourself the step.

DIRECTIONS

1. Prepare water bath canner, jars, and lids per steps on page 138.
2. Cut apples into quarters and remove the cores. Combine the apples and water in a large saucepan. Cook apples at a simmer until extremely soft, about 30 minutes. If needed, add additional water 1/2 cup at a time to keep the apples from burning. Remove from heat.
3. Blend the apples until smooth using an immersion blender. Then return the apples to medium heat.
4. Add the sugars, lemon juice, cinnamon, ginger, cloves, and nutmeg. Cook at a gentle boil over medium heat until the mixture reduces and is thickened enough to mound on a spoon. Stir frequently to prevent sticking.
5. Remove from heat. Ladle hot apple butter into a hot jar, leaving 1/4-inch headspace. Remove air bubbles and confirm proper headspace. Wipe the jar rim clean and center a flat lid on the jar. Apply the band and adjust to fingertip-tight. Place the jar in the boiling water canner. Repeat until all jars are filled.
6. Process jars for 15 minutes, adjusting time for altitude (see page 136). Turn off the heat, remove the canner lid, and let the jars stand for 5 minutes. Move the jars to a thick towel or wooden cutting board on the counter, and let them cool for 12-24 hours. Do not retighten any rings that have loosened.
7. Once cool, press on the center of each lid to make sure the jar is sealed properly—the lid should not flex at all when pressed.
8. Wipe down the jars and decorate as desired (see page 11 for ideas). Tie on the tags.

red onion jam

You're going to have to trust me on this one! I know it sounds weird, but this sweet and savory jam is *to die for* on top of burgers or on a fancy charcuterie board.

INGREDIENTS

- 2 pounds red onions, quartered and thinly sliced
- 1 1/2 cups port wine
- 1/2 cup red wine vinegar
- 2 teaspoons salt
- 1 teaspoon ground black pepper
- 1 teaspoon mustard seeds
- 1 cup cold water
- 3 tablespoons low-sugar powdered pectin
- 1/2 cup sugar

protip

It's important to use low-sugar/no-sugar pectin for this recipe because the low sugar content of the jam means it will not gel if you use regular pectin.

DIRECTIONS

1. Prepare water bath canner, jars, and lids per steps on page 138.
2. Combine the onions, port wine, red wine vinegar, salt, black pepper, and mustard seeds in a medium saucepan. Cook over medium heat for 15 minutes, or until onions are translucent, stirring occasionally.
3. Stir in the water and pectin. Stirring constantly, bring the onion mixture to a full rolling boil that cannot be stirred down.
4. Add sugar, stirring to dissolve. Return mixture to a full rolling boil. Boil hard for 1 minute, stirring constantly.
5. Turn off the burner and remove from the heat. Ladle hot jam into a hot jar, leaving a 1/4-inch headspace. Remove air bubbles and confirm proper headspace. Wipe the jar rim clean and center a flat lid on the jar. Apply the band and adjust to fingertip-tight. Place the jar in the boiling water canner. Repeat until all jars are filled.
6. Process jars 10 minutes, adjusting time for altitude (see page 136). Turn off the heat, remove the canner lid, and let the jars stand for 5 minutes. Move the jars to a thick towel or wooden cutting board on the counter, and let them cool for 12-24 hours. Do not retighten any rings that have loosened.
7. Once cool, press on the center of each lid to make sure the jar is sealed properly—the lid should not flex at all when pressed.
8. Wipe down the jars and decorate as desired (see page 11 for ideas). Tie on the tags.

Oktoberfest Mustard

100% HANDMADE · MADE WITH LOVE

Cranberry Mustard

Dijon Mustard

100% HANDMADE · MADE WITH LOVE

mustard flight

PLAN AHEAD

These need
2 TO 3 MONTHS
rest time

Have a mustard lover on your list? These recipes are for them! I have three homemade mustard options here that you can mix or match or do what I do—gift them as a sampler flight.

oktoberfest mustard

INGREDIENTS

- 1 1/2 cups beer
- 1/2 cup brown mustard seeds
- 1/2 cup yellow mustard seeds
- 1 cup water
- 1/2 cup malt vinegar
- 1/2 cup lightly packed brown sugar
- 1/2 cup dry mustard
- 1 tablespoon onion powder

protip

Right after cooking, don't be worried if your mustard is a little bitter. Mustard really needs to rest for at least 2 weeks in the jars before serving. For the best flavor, let the mustard rest for 2-3 months.

DIRECTIONS

1. In a saucepan, combine the beer and the mustard seeds. Bring to a boil over medium-high heat. Remove from heat, cover, and let stand for about 2 hours.
2. Prepare water bath canner, jars, and lids per steps on page 138.
3. In a blender, puree the seeds and any remaining liquid until most of the seeds are chopped up. You want it to be a little grainy.
4. Transfer the mixture back into the saucepan, and whisk in the water, vinegar, brown sugar, dry mustard, and onion powder. Stir frequently over high heat and bring to a boil. Reduce the heat to medium and boil gently, stirring frequently, until the volume is reduced by a third, about 15 minutes.
5. Ladle the hot mustard into the jars, leaving 1/4-inch headspace. Remove air bubbles and adjust headspace if needed. Wipe the jar rim clean and center a flat lid on the jar. Apply the band and adjust to fingertip-tight. Place the jar in the boiling water canner. Repeat until all jars are filled.
6. Boil jars for 10 minutes, adjusting time for altitude (see page 136). Turn off the heat, remove the canner lid, and let the jars stand for 5 minutes. Move the jars to a thick towel or wooden cutting board on the counter, and let them cool for 12-24 hours. Do not retighten any rings that have loosened.
7. Once cool, press on the center of each lid to make sure the jar is sealed properly—the lid should not flex at all when pressed.
8. Wipe down the jars and decorate as desired (see page 11 for ideas). Tie on the tags.

cranberry mustard

INGREDIENTS

- 1 cup red wine vinegar
- 2/3 cup yellow mustard seeds
- 2 3/4 cups fresh or frozen cranberries (1 12-oz bag)
- 1 cup water
- 1 tablespoon Worcestershire sauce
- 3/4 cup sugar
- 1/4 cup dry mustard
- 1 teaspoon ground allspice

DIRECTIONS

1. Bring vinegar to a boil in a medium saucepan. Remove from heat and add mustard seeds. Cover and let stand at room temperature until seeds have absorbed most of the vinegar, about 1 1/2 hours.
2. Prepare water bath canner, jars, and lids per steps on page 138.
3. Combine mustard seeds and remaining liquid with cranberries, water, and Worcestershire sauce in a blender. Process until smooth.
4. Bring mustard mixture to a boil in a medium saucepan, stirring often. Whisk in sugar, dry mustard, and allspice. Continue to simmer, stirring frequently, until volume is reduced by a third, about 15 minutes.
5. Ladle the hot mustard into a hot jar, leaving a 1/4-inch headspace. Remove air bubbles and confirm proper headspace. Wipe the jar rim clean and center a flat lid on the jar. Apply the band and adjust to fingertip-tight. Place the jar in the boiling water canner. Repeat until all jars are filled.
6. Process jars 10 minutes, adjusting time for altitude (see page 136). Turn off the heat, remove the canner lid, and let the jars stand for 5 minutes. Move the jars to a thick towel or wooden cutting board on the counter, and let them cool for 12-24 hours. Do not retighten any rings that have loosened.
7. Once cool, press on the center of each lid to make sure the jar sealed properly—the lid should not flex at all when pressed.
8. Wipe down the jars and decorate as desired (see page 11 for ideas). Tie on the tags.

protip

Yellow mustard seeds are milder than brown mustard seeds. I recommend them here so as not to overpower the cranberry flavor, but if you want a stronger mustard flavor and bite, you can use half yellow and half brown seeds.

dijon mustard

INGREDIENTS

- 2 cups chopped onion
- 2 cups dry white wine
- 1 cup white wine vinegar
- 6 garlic cloves, coarsely chopped
- 4 black peppercorns
- 1 sprig of fresh rosemary
- 1 teaspoon salt
- 1 cup yellow mustard seeds
- ⅓ cup dry mustard
- 2 ⅔ cups water

DIRECTIONS

1. Combine onion, wine, vinegar, garlic, peppercorns, rosemary, and salt in a large saucepan. Bring to a boil over high heat. Reduce heat and simmer, uncovered and stirring occasionally, for 15 to 20 minutes, or until the onion is very soft.
2. Remove from heat. Strain the onion mixture through a wire-mesh strainer into a bowl. Discard solids.
3. Stir mustard seeds and dry mustard into the strained liquid. Cover and let stand at room temperature for 24 hours.
4. Prepare water bath canner, jars, and lids per steps on page 138.
5. Process mustard in a blender or food processor and add the water. Blend until very smooth. The mustard will be slightly thin.
6. Transfer mustard to a small saucepan. Bring to a boil, stirring often. Reduce heat and simmer uncovered for 5 minutes, or until thickened slightly.
7. Ladle hot mustard into a hot jar, leaving 1/4-inch headspace. Remove air bubbles and confirm proper headspace. Wipe the jar rim clean and center a flat lid on the jar. Apply the band and adjust to fingertip-tight. Place the jar in the boiling water canner. Repeat until all jars are filled.
8. Boil jars 10 minutes, adjusting time for altitude (see page 136). Turn off the heat, remove the canner lid, and let the jars stand for 5 minutes. Move the jars to a thick towel or wooden cutting board on the counter, and let them cool for 12-24 hours. Do not retighten any rings that have loosened.
9. Once cool, press on the center of each lid to make sure the jar is sealed properly—the lid should not flex at all when pressed.
10. Wipe down the jars and decorate as desired (see page 11 for ideas). Tie on the tags.

pickled beets

It doesn't matter if you are a beet-lover or a beet-hater, everyone seems to enjoy these pickled beets! They are sweet, tangy, and have that amazing pickle zing that you are used to from cucumber pickles. I love serving these on a charcuterie board or just eating them straight from the jar!

INGREDIENTS

- 4 pounds beets (about 20-24 medium size beets, 1 to 1 1/2 inches in diameter)
- 2 1/2 cups apple cider vinegar
- 2 cups sugar
- 1 1/2 cups water
- 3 cinnamon sticks
- 1 tablespoon whole mustard seeds
- 1 teaspoon whole allspice
- 1 teaspoon whole cloves
- 1 teaspoon pickling salt
- 3 cups thinly sliced onions (about 3 medium)
- 4 sprigs of fresh rosemary

DIRECTIONS

1. Prepare water bath canner, jars, and lids per steps on page 138.
2. Wash beets and trim off the leaves, leaving about 2" of stem.
3. Place trimmed beets in a large saucepan and cover with water by at least 1 inch. Bring to a boil over high heat.
4. Cook until beets are just tender—about 20-30 minutes depending on the size. Then drain and allow beets to cool. Once beets are cool to the touch, trim off roots and stem, peel, and slice into 1/4" to 1/2" thick slices.
5. In a large saucepan, combine the vinegar, sugar, water, cinnamon sticks, mustard seeds, allspice, cloves, and salt. Bring to a boil, then reduce heat and simmer for about 5 minutes, stirring occasionally. Add in the beets and onion, and cook until the beets are warmed through, about 5 additional minutes. Reduce heat to low, and remove and discard the cinnamon sticks.
6. Pack hot beets into the prepared hot jars, leaving a 1/2-inch headspace. Pack a single rosemary sprig into each jar. Then ladle the hot pickling liquid over the beets, again leaving a 1/2 inch headspace.
7. Remove air bubbles and confirm proper headspace. Wipe the jar rim clean and center a flat lid on the jar. Apply the band and adjust to fingertip-tight. Place the jar in the boiling water canner. Repeat until all jars are filled.
8. Boil jars 30 minutes, adjusting time for altitude (see page 136). Turn off the heat, remove the canner lid, and let the jars stand for 5 minutes. Move the jars to a thick towel or wooden cutting board on the counter, and let them cool for 12-24 hours. Do not retighten any rings that have loosened.
9. Once cool, press on the center of each lid to make sure the jar is sealed properly—the lid should not flex at all when pressed.
10. Wipe down the jars and decorate as desired (see page 11 for ideas). Tie on the tags.

HANDMADE WITH

RICH AND FUDGY

Brownies

INSTRUCTIONS: Preheat oven to 350°F. Line a 9" x 9" pan with parchment paper or aluminum foil, spray liberally with cooking spray. Set aside. In a medium mixing bowl, combine 2 cups of the brownie mix with 1/2 cup melted butter or oil, 2 eggs, and 1 teaspoon vanilla extract. Stir until well combined. Spread into the prepared pan and bake in a preheated oven for 20-25 minutes, or until a toothpick inserted about an inch away from the edge of the pan comes out mostly clean. Let cool completely before removing from pan and slicing into squares.

acknowledgements

A project like this is never accomplished alone, and I'd like to express my deepest thanks to everyone who helped get this book from idea to reality.

I'll kick off with a special thanks to Julie Grice for being my editor, confidante, project manager, right-hand-woman, and regular cat herder (I am the cat). You know this book wouldn't exist without you. I appreciate you.

To my parents: thank you for teaching me how to cook at a young age and for being my very first taste testers—hopefully the food tastes better now than it did when I was five!

To my friends: thank you for always being there when I need a good laugh or to talk about something non-food related (let's be honest, it's mostly motorsports). You all bring me so much joy and perspective. Thanks for being in my life.

To my husband: thank you for doing all the dishes and being the best taste tester a girl could ever ask for. I appreciate all the ways big and small you work to make our lives better. I am so lucky to have you by my side on this wild journey.

To my daughter: thank you for always having a hug ready for me—hug power gets me through my day! I am so proud to be your Mama. P.S. I hid 11 tiny race cars like this one in this book. Have fun finding them! Meow.

To everyone who read this book: thank you for spending your precious time with me and my ideas. I am so grateful for you.

Until next time!

♡ Cassie

about the author

Cassie Johnston is a holistic nutritionist, recipe developer, and all-around food lover who has been sharing her award-winning recipes on her website Wholefully since 2010. She loves dark chocolate, homegrown tomatoes, motorsports, and anything that sparkles. She lives in Indiana with her family on a small homestead.

Other Titles By Cassie

- *Cooking with Greek Yogurt*
- *Chia, Quinoa, Kale, Oh My!*

Find more from Cassie at **wholefully.com** and **growfully.com**

index

ALCOHOL

Bloody Mary Cocktail Kit 88-89
Bourbon Peach Jam 142-143
Coffee Liqueur 82-83
Coffee Martini Cocktail Kit 89
Cranberry Liqueur 84-85
Irish Cream 90-91
Limoncello 86-87
Margarita Cocktail Kit 89
Moscow Mule Cocktail Kit 89
Old Fashioned Cocktail Kit 89
Tequila Sunrise Cocktail Kit 89
Vanilla Extract 102-103

ALMONDS

Cranberry and Pistachio Trail Mix 46-47
Nuts 'n' Bolts 52-53
Rosemary Party Nuts 42-43
Sweet and Spicy Mixed Nuts 44-45

BAKED GOODS

Brownie Mix 18-19
Cheese Straws 48-49
Cookie Mix Gifts 15
Confetti Cake Mix 24-25
Cranberry Orange Muffin Mix 20-21
Double Chocolate Muffin Mix 22-23
Gingerbread Cookie Mix 26-27
Gluten-Free Chocolate Chip Cookie Mix 32-33
M&M Cookie Mix 28-29
Snickerdoodle Cookie Mix 30-31

BAKING INGREDIENTS

Cinnamon Sugar 108-109
Citrus Sugar 108-109
Espresso Sugar 108-109
Ginger Sugar 108-109
Lavender Sugar 108-109
Vanilla Extract 102-103
Vanilla Sugar 108-109

BEANS AND LENTILS

Coconut Curry Soup Mix 116-117
Five-Bean Soup Mix 126-127
Kidney Bean Safety 125, 127
Roasted Chickpeas 50-51
Black Bean Soup Mix 118-119
Split Pea Soup Mix 120-121
Three-Bean Chili Mix 124-125

BREAKFAST

Berry Syrups 140-141
Cranberry Orange Muffin Mix 20-21
Double Chocolate Muffin Mix 22-23
Gluten-Free Pancake Mix 36-37
Peanut Butter Chocolate Chip Granola 64-65
Whole Grain Pancake Mix 34-35

CANDIES

Buckeyes 66-67
Cranberry Pistachio Bark 62-63
Peppermint Bark 58-59
Sea Salt Honey Caramels 56-57
Turtles 68-69

CANNING

Adjusting for Altitude 136
Berry Syrups 140-141
Bourbon Peach Jam 142-143
Cranberry Mustard 150, 152
Dijon Mustard 150, 153
Oktoberfest Mustard 150-151
Pickled Beets 154-155
Pomegranate Jelly 144-145
Red Onion Jam 148-149
Shelf Life 136
Spiced Apple Butter 146-147
Tools Needed 136
Water Bath Canning Step-by-Step 138-139

CASHEWS

Classic Trail Mix 46-47
Nuts 'n' Bolts 52-53
Rosemary Party Nuts 42-43
Sweet and Spicy Mixed Nuts 44-45

CEREAL

Nuts 'n' Bolts 52-53
Puppy Chow 70-71

CHOCOLATE

Brownie Mix 18-19
Buckeyes 66-67
Cappuccino Mix 74-75
Classic Trail Mix 46-47
Cranberry Pistachio Bark 62-63
Double Chocolate Muffin Mix 22-23
Edible Cookie Dough 60-61
Gluten-Free Chocolate Chip Cookie Mix 32-33
Hot Cocoa Mix 80-81
Irish Cream 90-91
M&M Cookie Mix 28-29
Peanut Butter Chocolate Chip Granola 64-65
Peanut Butter Lovers' Trail Mix 46-47
Peppermint Bark 58-59
Puppy Chow 70-71
Turtles 68-69

CHOCOLATE, WHITE

Cranberry and Pistachio Trail Mix 46-47
Cranberry Pistachio Bark 62-63
Peppermint Bark 58-59

CHRISTMAS

Cranberry Liqueur 84-85
Hot Cocoa Mix 80-81
Gingerbread Cookie Mix 26-27
Peppermint Bark 58-59

CINNAMON

Cinnamon Sugar 108-109
Cinnamon Sugar Popcorn Seasoning 40-41
Gingerbread Cookie Mix 26-27
Golden Milk Mix 76-77
Loose Leaf Chai 78-79
Snickerdoodle Cookie Mix 30-31
Spiced Apple Butter 146-147

CITRUS

Bloody Mary Cocktail Kit 88-89
Chile Lime Olive Oil 106-107
Chipotle and Lime Finishing Salt 100-101
Citrus Sugar 108-109
Lemon and Thyme Finishing Salt 100-101
Limoncello 86-87
Margarita Cocktail Kit 89
Moscow Mule Cocktail Kit 89
Old Fashioned Cocktail Kit 89
Tequila Sunrise Cocktail Kit 89

COFFEE

Cappuccino Mix 74-75
Coffee Liqueur 82-83
Coffee Martini Cocktail Kit 89
Espresso Sugar 108-109
Irish Cream 90-91

CONDIMENTS

Berry Syrups 140-141
Bourbon Peach Jam 142-143
Cranberry Mustard 150, 152
Dijon Mustard 150, 153
Oktoberfest Mustard 150-151
Pomegranate Jelly 144-145
Quick Hot Sauce 110-111
Ranch Seasoning and Dressing Mix 98-99
Red Onion Jam 148-149
Spiced Apple Butter 146-147

COOKIES

Cookie Mix Gifts 15
Edible Cookie Dough 60-61
Gingerbread Cookie Mix 26-27
Gluten-Free Chocolate Chip Cookie Mix 32-33
M&M Cookie Mix 28-29
Snickerdoodle Cookie Mix 30-31

CRANBERRIES

Cranberry and Pistachio Trail Mix 46-47
Cranberry Liqueur 84-85
Cranberry Mustard 150, 152
Cranberry Orange Muffin Mix 20-21
Cranberry Pistachio Bark 62-63

DRINKS, READY-TO-DRINK

Coffee Liqueur 82-83
Cranberry Liqueur 84-85
Irish Cream 90-91
Limoncello 86-87

DRINK MIXES

Cappuccino Mix 74-75
Golden Milk Mix 76-77
Hot Cocoa Mix 80-81
Loose Leaf Chai 78-79

DRY MIXES

Black Bean Soup Mix 118-119
Brownie Mix 18-19
Cappuccino Mix 74-75
Chicken Noodle Soup Mix 122-13
Coconut Curry Soup Mix 116-117
Confetti Cake Mix 24-25
Cranberry Orange Muffin Mix 20-21
Double Chocolate Muffin Mix 22-23
Five-Bean Soup Mix 126-127
Garlic and Herb Pizza Crust Mix 130-131
Gingerbread Cookie Mix 26-27
Gluten-Free Chocolate Chip Cookie Mix 32-33
Gluten-Free Pancake Mix 36-37
Gluten-Free Pizza Crust Mix 132-133
Golden Milk Mix 76-77
Hot Cocoa Mix 80-81
Italian Barley Soup Mix 128-129
M&M Cookie Mix 28-29
Ranch Seasoning and Dressing Mix 98-99
Snickerdoodle Cookie Mix 30-31
Split Pea Soup Mix 120-121
Three-Bean Chili Mix 124-125
Whole Grain Pancake Mix 34-35

FRUIT also see individual fruits

Berry Syrups 140-141
Bourbon Peach Jam 142-143
Citrus Sugar 108-109
Cranberry Liqueur 84-85
Cranberry Mustard 150, 152
Cranberry Orange Muffin Mix 20-21
Cranberry Pistachio Bark 62-63
Limoncello 86-87
Pomegranate Jelly 144-145
Spiced Apple Butter 146-147

GARLIC

Basil and Sun-Dried Tomato Olive Oil 106-107
Garlic and Herb Pizza Crust Mix 130-131
Peeled Garlic 112-113
Quick Hot Sauce 110-11
Rosemary and Garlic Olive Oil 106-107

GINGER

Bourbon Peach Jam 142-143
Gingerbread Cookie Mix 26-27
Ginger Sugar 108-109
Golden Milk Mix 76-77
Loose Leaf Chai 78-79
Spiced Apple Butter 146-147

INFUSIONS

Basil and Sun-Dried Tomato Olive Oil 106-107
Chile Lime Olive Oil 106-107
Chipotle and Lime Finishing Salt 100-101
Cinnamon Sugar 108-109
Citrus Sugar 108-109
Coffee Liqueur 82-83
Cranberry Liqueur 84-85
Espresso Sugar 108-109
Ginger Sugar 108-109
Lavender Sugar 108-109
Lemon and Thyme Finishing Salt 100-101
Limoncello 86-87
Peeled Garlic 112-113
Rosemary and Garlic Olive Oil 106-107
Sage and Rosemary Finishing Salt 100-101
Vanilla Extract 102-103
Vanilla Sugar 108-109

JARS

Etiquette 9
Lids 10
Sizes 6
Sourcing 9
Wrapping Ideas 11-15

MUFFINS

Cranberry Orange Muffin Mix 20-21
Double Chocolate Muffin Mix 22-23

OATS

M&M Cookie Mix 28-29
Peanut Butter Chocolate Chip Granola 64-65
Whole Grain Pancake Mix 34-35

PEANUT BUTTER

Buckeyes 66-67
Peanut Butter Chocolate Chip Granola 64-65
Peanut Butter Lovers' Trail Mix 46-47
Puppy Chow 70-71

PEANUTS

Classic Trail Mix 46-47
Nuts 'n' Bolts 52-53
Peanut Butter Chocolate Chip Granola 64-65
Peanut Butter Lovers' Trail Mix 46-47
Rosemary Party Nuts 42-43

PECANS

Gluten-Free Chocolate Chip Cookie Mix 32-33
Rosemary Party Nuts 42-43
Sweet and Spicy Mixed Nuts 44-45
Turtles 68-69

PEPPERS

Chipotle and Lime Finishing Salt 100-101
Chile Lime Olive Oil 106-107
Quick Hot Sauce 110-111

PISTACHIOS

Cranberry and Pistachio Trail Mix 46-47
Cranberry Pistachio Bark 62-63
Rosemary Party Nuts 42-43

PIZZA

Garlic and Herb Pizza Crust Mix 130-131
Gluten-Free Pizza Crust Mix 132-133
Pizza Night Gift Basket 15

ROSEMARY

Chicken Noodle Soup Mix 122-123
Dijon Mustard 150, 153
Pickled Beets 154-155
Rosemary and Garlic Olive Oil 106-107
Rosemary Party Nuts 42-43
Sage and Rosemary Finishing Salt 100-101

SAVORY INGREDIENTS

Barbecue Spice Rub 94-95
Basil and Sun-Dried Tomato Olive Oil 106-107
Chile Lime Olive Oil 106-107
Chipotle and Lime Finishing Salt 100-101
Cranberry Mustard 150, 152
Dijon Mustard 150, 153
Everything Bagel Seasoning 96-97
Fish and Chicken Grill Seasoning 94-95
Lemon and Thyme Finishing Salt 100-101
Oktoberfest Mustard 150-151
Peeled Garlic 112-113
Quick Hot Sauce 110-111
Ranch Seasoning and Dressing Mix 98-99
Rosemary and Garlic Olive Oil 106-107
Sage and Rosemary Finishing Salt 100-101
Sun-Dried Tomatoes 104-105

SEASONINGS

Barbecue Spice Rub 94-95
Chipotle and Lime Finishing Salt 100-101
Cinnamon Sugar Popcorn Seasoning 40-41
Dill Pickle Popcorn Seasoning 40-41
Everything Bagel Seasoning 96-97
Fish and Chicken Grill Seasoning 94-95
Lemon and Thyme Finishing Salt 100-101
Ranch Popcorn Seasoning 40-41
Ranch Seasoning and Dressing Mix 98-99
Sage and Rosemary Finishing Salt 100-101

SNACKS, READY-TO-EAT

Buckeyes 66-67
Cheese Straws 48-49
Classic Trail Mix 46-47
Cranberry and Pistachio Trail Mix 46-47
Cranberry Pistachio Bark 62-63
Edible Cookie Dough 60-61
Movie Night Gift Basket 15
Nuts 'n' Bolts 52-53
Peanut Butter Chocolate Chip Granola 64-65
Peanut Butter Lovers' Trail Mix 46-47
Peppermint Bark 58-59
Pickled Beets 154-155
Puppy Chow 70-71
Roasted Chickpeas 50-51
Rosemary Party Nuts 42-43
Sea Salt Honey Caramels 56-57
Sweet and Spicy Mixed Nuts 44-45
Turtles 68-69

SOUPS

Black Bean Soup Mix 118-119
Chicken Noodle Soup Mix 122-123
Chili Night Gift Basket 15
Coconut Curry Soup Mix 116-117
Five-Bean Soup Mix 126-127
Italian Barley Soup Mix 128-129
Split Pea Soup Mix 120-121
Three-Bean Chili Mix 124-125

SUN-DRIED TOMATOES

Basil and Sun-Dried Tomato Olive Oil 106-107
Italian Barley Soup Mix 128-129
Sun-Dried Tomatoes 104-105

TAGS

Downloading and Printing 14

THYME

Chicken Noodle Soup Mix 122-123
Lemon and Thyme Finishing Salt 100-101
Rosemary Party Nuts 42-43

TURMERIC

Dill Pickle Popcorn Seasoning 40-41
Fish and Chicken Grill Seasoning 94-95
Golden Milk Mix 76-77

VANILLA

Coffee Liqueur 82-83
Golden Milk Mix 76-77
Vanilla Extract 102-103
Vanilla Sugar 108-109

WALNUTS

Brownie Mix 18-19
Gluten-Free Chocolate Chip Cookie Mix 32-33
Rosemary Party Nuts 42-43
Sweet and Spicy Mixed Nuts 44-45

WRAPPING

Fabric Circles 12
Gift Baskets 15
Ribbon or Twine 11
Tea Towel 13